"Mary Haskett's journey is one that none of us would choose! Her captivating account of it, however, sweeps the reader up in the experience, as her extraordinary ability to portray details engages all the senses. A surprising story, from life as an abandoned inter-racial child in an English convent, to choices that marked the direction of her adult life, to the encounter with grace that shaped all that follows."

ETHEL ROWNTREE
Publisher and Editor, *Beyond Ordinary Living* magazine

"Mary Haskett tells a story of brokenness—scandal, violation, betrayal—the pain of being human that touches us all. But hers, and ours, is also a story of redemption, of healing. As she recounts her life with candor and engaging prose, Haskett opens a window to the divine and gives us hope."

MARGARET BUCHANAN
Author, *Parenting with Purpose*, Baker Book House, 2004

"An obviously gifted story-teller, Mary writes this riveting account of her own life with heart-warming honesty, charming humor, and great doses of grace. In all of it—her birth in unusual circumstances, her childhood joys and struggles in war-torn England, her great loves and painful disappointments, and her inspiring walk with her Best Friend—there is never a dull moment. Mary has given us a great treasure: A beautiful story, beautifully told."

FAY ROWE
Author of *What's In a Name* and *Keepers of the Testimony*

"From the first page, you'll be swept away on the incredible journey that has been Mary Haskett's life. She shows us over and over how God sees and cares for his children—even when we think He is silent. *Reverend Mother's Daughter* is a wonderful read. I know you'll be blessed."

GINGER KOLBABA
Author, *Desperate Pastors' Wives*
Editor, *Marriage Partnership* magazine

"The story of Mary Haskett's life is a captivating one. Her book is difficult to put down. I found myself there, in wartime, sharing the experiences and the people alongside her. An excellent and truly inspiring book!"

DONNA FAWCETT
Author of *Thriving in the Home School* and Donna Dawson novels *Redeemed* and *The Adam and Eve Project*

Reverend MOTHER'S Daughter

Reverend
MOTHER'S
A REAL LIFE STORY
Daughter

Mary Haskett

BELIEVE BOOKS
Life Stories That Inspire
WASHINGTON, DC

REVEREND MOTHER'S DAUGHTER
By Mary Haskett

Reverend Mother's Daughter is a real life story. Some names and places, however, have been changed to protect individual privacy.

ISBN: 0-9787428-1-8

Library of Congress Control Number: 2007906054

Cover design: *Jack Kotowicz, Washington, DC, VelocityDesignGroup.com*
Layout design: *Annie Kotowicz*
Photo scanning: *Andrew Schulz, www.images.on.ca*

Believe Books publishes the inspirational life stories of extraordinary believers in God from around the world. Requests for information should be addressed to **Believe Books** at www.believebooks.com. **Believe Books** is a registered trade name of **Believe Books, LLC** of Washington, DC.

Printed in the United States of America

Dedicated to my Reverend Mother

CONTENTS

FOREWORD

I first met Mary Testolin Haskett in 1993 when I became the senior pastor of Royal View Church in London, Ontario. Immediately I was impressed by Mary's love for Christ and her compassion for people.

A faithful and active member of Royal View for many years, Mary provided leadership to women's ministries and singles groups, teaching Bible classes and doing prayer counseling. As a single mom, she took special interest in people who had experienced the pain of divorce and in an effort to help them, she developed a ministry for single parents. With a positive approach, the singles group's motto was "Singled out to Serve." Mary also administered "Just Me and the Kids," an in-depth program that helped single parents and their families through the pain of separation.

In the mid 1990's, Mary joined the pastoral staff of Royal View Church as Minister of Visitation. Her warm personality and genuine love for people endeared her to many in the congregation. Her wisdom, insight and attention to detail were a tremendous help to me as pastor. In 2002, she married a wonderful man by the name of Allan Haskett and began a new chapter in her life as Mary Haskett.

Mary always had a flair for writing; many times she left a poem, a reflection or a short story on my desk. The richness of her words expressed her heart and the experiences of her own personal journey. A woman of determination and faith, her zest for life overflows in her writings. They are an inspiration to everyone who reads them.

My friendship with Mary Haskett is something I treasure. She has been a tremendous blessing to me and to my wife Judy and our three children. It is an honor for me to commend Mary's first book—her amazing life story—to you. I am confident that you will be inspired and blessed by it.

GARRY B. FESS
Senior Pastor, Royal View Church
London, ON

ACKNOWLEDGEMENTS

With heartfelt gratitude to my dear husband Allan, who has encouraged me to recognize my worth as a child of the King; to my sister and friend Hazil, who traveled much of this journey with me; to my dear children Michael, David, Christopher and Daniela for their constant encouragement; and to Dianne and Kelsey who refer to me as "Mother Mary." I embrace you and the rest of my family and many friends with love.

Many thanks also to my writing friends for their support and enthusiasm.

1

Family

"I don't want the family to know about you." My sister's voice shook a little. She sat in her wheelchair in the visitor's room of the nursing home a tiny 91-year-old woman shrunken with age. Her son John sat beside her. I looked at my sister who was twenty-two years older than me and swallowed hard. "Why?" I asked.

"Well" she said, "Mother had a wonderful personality and our family held her in high regard. I want them all to remember her that way. Your birth devastated poor daddy, seeing you—a brown baby, what a shock for him. The family doesn't know about you and it's best they never do. Mummy tried to have an abortion, but her doctor told her she was too far along with the pregnancy."

I digested this news in silence and then spoke to my sister—protesting her decision.

"But I exist and they are my family too! I have a right to know them and they have a right to know me." My husband, who sat next to me, took my hand and squeezed it.

"Mary has searched for you for many years," he said.

Yes, I thought. My mind flew back to the day when I came in from shopping. I remembered Allan's excitement: "Guess what, we've had a call from the Salvation Army—they think they've found your family." Sixteen months had gone by since I'd sent them my file and it was now September 2002. He went on to say someone had talked to my sister and she had asked one question.

"Is Mary of African descent? If she is then she's my sister."

I had not forgotten the exhilaration of the moment. At last— almost three years of intensive searching had finally brought answers. Our visit resulted from several phone calls to my sister's son, John, who expressed disbelief at the news of his grandma's secret. Later that month, Allan and I had driven from Canada, crossing the border at Buffalo and taking Interstate 90 east all the way to Utica, New York. During our long drive I shared with Allan that I had moments of excitement and moments of doubt. My sister had not been pleased when I called her at the nursing home. With her very British accent, she had said, "Now Mary I don't want you calling here. You must only talk to John on his cell phone." And here we were and I understood—she was insisting I remain an unknown to my family.

"At least will you tell me about my father?" I said.

My sister's face lit up and she sighed a little, "A tall handsome young man I must say. He came from West Africa to study law. Mummy and Daddy were involved in many ministries; they helped students from Africa and the West Indies to find accommodation near the London University. Sometimes they had them stay in their home and I'm afraid that's when your father had a relationship with Mother."

"Did my father know about me?"

"Oh, yes. After Daddy saw you, he went to the house and told that young man to leave immediately." My sister sighed and stared at the floor; she had a faraway look in her eyes. She looked up suddenly. "I became pregnant with John at the same time." She patted her son's knee. "Mummy was nearly 40 and I just twenty-two. It was very hard for me too."

"Yes I can believe that," I said, "but I believe in God and I think He has allowed me to find you for a reason."

John spoke. "Are you religious? My eldest son is religious too."

My heart skipped a beat. "Where does he go to church?" I asked.

"He's a Reverend," John said. "He has his own church not far from here."

"Perhaps we could go to his church on Sunday," my husband suggested.

"No," my sister said. "It's best not to."

Suddenly John pulled out his cell phone, dialed a number and said to the person on the other end. "I have someone here I think you should talk to." He thrust the phone at me and I took it, covering the mouthpiece.

"Is it your son?" I asked. He nodded. "Can I tell him who I am?"

"No, no." They both whispered in unison, at the same time shaking their heads vigorously.

God, give me wisdom, I prayed as I put the phone to my ear.

I cleared my throat. "Hello, I'm pleased to meet you," I said. "My husband and I are visiting with your grandma." *Please don't ask me who I am*, I thought, and before he could, I asked, "How are you?"

"I'm well," he said cautiously.

"I understand you're a pastor?" Giving him no time to reply I blurted out, "I believe in God too."

Now he cleared his throat. "Well that's nice," he said.

I pulled a tissue from my purse and wiped my forehead. "Um, where did you go to college?"

Polite, but obviously puzzled by this strange phone call he told me the name of his college. I thought, *I need to bring this conversation to an end.*

"Well it's been nice meeting you if only over the phone. I'm here with my husband and I know he's ready for dinner." I attempted a laugh.

"Yes, you have a good evening. Goodbye."

A little annoyed at being pushed into this unexpected dialogue, I handed the phone back to John. But one piece of information that his son had divulged resonated with me—I had some very dear friends whose daughters had attended that same college.

The visit over, Allan and I returned to Canada. I cherished the information about my great-nephew. *Would God allow us to meet one day?* I wondered.

2

Mystery Baby

On August the 25th, 1934, Mr. Cattermole drove his black Rolls Royce along High Street and into the tiny village of Thames Ditton, in Surrey, England. The car's purring changed as the wheels met with the gravel driveway of the large house. Mr. Cattermole glanced at the shrubberies to his left and caught glimpses of the walkways between the rich foliage. Beyond lay the low red brick buildings that in days past had housed horses and carriages; but now converted into a priory, these buildings served as living quarters for the Sisters of Mercy, a small order of Anglican nuns who owned the property.

Mr. Cattermole smiled; he visualized the sisters hurrying silently along the cloister with its smooth stone floor. The long passageway ran inside the length of the building from the nuns' quarters and then took a right turn to the main house. The nuns always walked softly and silently through the cloister, either entering the chapel for service, or going to the wards to care for the aged. But on this day, Mr. Cattermole knew a great change was afoot. He continued along the driveway, glancing at the outer wall of the red brick chapel that stood in all its majesty with its stained-glass windows winking in the bright sun.

To his right, stately trees stood on manicured lawns that swept away and curved around to the back of the house. Roses of every hue spilled out of the flowerbed in the center of the driveway; their heady perfume wafted through his car window.

He brought his car to a halt, quickly alighted and saw the sisters excitedly chatting to one another in front of the cloister doors. He smiled again as he opened the passenger door of the car; Eva Mary, Reverend Mother Superior, wriggled forward in her seat.

"Would you?" she said, holding a tiny brown baby up to him. He touched the peak of his cap and obliged. He looked down at the baby and smiled as a pair of solemn brown eyes stared up at him. The sisters and a number of staff appeared in the doorway, eager to see the baby. They knew of its coming, but not its circumstances. "Come along my little pet," Reverend Mother said as she retrieved the baby.

Mr. Cattermole returned to the car and drove back down the driveway. In all his years of service to the Reverend Mother, this had to have been the most extraordinary trip. He shook his head. "My, my," he said to himself as he picked up speed on High Street.

Dorothy, Reverend Mother's personal maid, held the door open and Reverend Mother, a tall regal figure, stepped inside, crossed the passageway and went through another set of doors into the cool interior of the great hall. She walked quickly over the ancient flagstone floor, veered to the right past the sweeping stone staircase and on into her private rooms. Dorothy followed her and others hovered in the doorway.

"Come and see her," Reverend Mother said, as she sat down in her high back floral chair. Sister Faith, a diminutive nun, walked across the room with arms outstretched.

"May I, Mother?" she said.

Reverend Mother chuckled, holding the baby closer. "Isn't she a darling?" She gazed intently at the child, taking in the black curls and the soft curve of her cheeks and the tiny fingers curled around her own. "You're my Mary," she announced to the baby, "and you're going to live here till you're all grown up." She held the baby up to Sister Faith. "We'll have our home for children yet," she said.

In that same year, on August 19, 1934, Adolph Hitler became Führer of Germany. From then on his fanaticism swept across Europe. Country after country surrendered to the Nazis. Hatred toward God's chosen people escalated; concentration camps were established and men became insane. Chaos reigned all over the world. By August 1940, the Germans began bombing offensives against airfields and factories in England. Daylight raids over Britain and concentrated attacks on central London increased, culminating in the German blitz of September 1940.

3

The Tunnel

August 1940:

"Mary, wake up." Hillary's whispers penetrated my sleepy state. I could hear the urgent wail of the sirens and I knew we had to go to the tunnel again. I rubbed my eyes as eleven-year-old Hillary pushed my feet into my shoes and pulled on my dressing gown. She lifted me out of my bed and set me down. A dim light from the landing penetrated the darkness. Others coaxed children from their cots and beds. I followed Hillary, a routine exercise for me now. I yawned and stretched as she lifted Ann, a girl the same age as me, out of her bed, and helped her with her gown and shoes. "Come on," Hillary said, grabbing my hand. Sister St. Claire, a round plump figure, counted heads as we went by. Along with others, we hurried down the stairs through the big kitchen with its scrubbed wooden floor and out of the back door. The siren's persistent wailing drowned out the cries of the babies as our procession hastily made its way across the walled courtyard. Tall trees swayed above us as if urging us to take shelter. Searchlights swept the night sky as we descended a flight of flag stone steps into the tunnel.

A variety of camp beds, deck chairs, and armchairs served as makeshift beds and lined each wall of the tunnel. We reached our designated sleeping spots and I climbed onto the deckchair that I shared with Hillary. She came and sat beside me. "I hope you won't wet," she said. "You're nearly six years old now and you shouldn't still be wetting." I didn't say anything, because I knew that I would.

From the other end of the tunnel Mr. Morgan, the warden, appeared wearing his long dark coat and warden's helmet. He strode down the tunnel and stopped at the entrance through which we had come. He grasped a thick wooden rod attached to the wall and pulled—a black felt curtain swished across the entrance blotting out the bright searchlights and dulling the noise of the sirens.

Mr. Morgan placed an electric heater at the entrance so that its warm rays pierced the tunnel's damp interior.

Nellie, the cook, had already lit one solitary lamp perched on a small table halfway down. "Are you ready then?" she asked. There were squeals of delight and we all chanted, "Yes." Nellie made us forget the inconveniences of the nightly interruptions; she started ladling hot cocoa into enamel mugs. Two maids moved down the narrow passage with the mugs on trays. I hoped Ada wouldn't come our way, but she did and she glared at me.

"You shouldn't have any chocolate," she hissed. "You dirty little bed wetter." She handed the mug to Hillary and I took it from her. As I sipped the drink I heard Sister St. Claire talking to Reverend Mother.

"They're all accounted for," she said. They came closer and I could see Reverend Mother nodding and interjecting. She saw me, bent down and gave me a kiss. The silver cross that she wore around her neck brushed my cheek.

"Finish your drink and go back to sleep, my darling," she said. "Take care of my Mary," she said to Hillary, as she ruffled my curls. I loved the fact that I was her Mary. I didn't know why, but she always said that to visitors and sometimes that made me a little smug. She walked away, saying, "I better get back, Sister." I knew that meant back to the big house where she looked after old people. I watched the light of my life walk away then I turned and saw Ada watching me with hatred in her eyes.

4

Where They
Won't Find Us

September 1940:

Sister St. Claire, Sister Faith, and Sister Monica—with help from some of the maids—stacked trunks, suitcases, and boxes in the hallway of St. Agnes Home for Children. All of the children who had relatives crowded into the second playroom, visiting and saying goodbye. Some of the men looked impressive in their smart uniforms. Reverend Mother had told us that we were going away to Torquay, in the south of England, a place where the Germans couldn't find us.

I ran up and down in the large playroom with Ann. We were both nearing our sixth birthday. Hazil, two years and nine months old, sat in her high chair alongside two other little ones in high chairs. They screeched with laughter as we ran back and forth. Each time I ran to Hazil first, planting a kiss on her cheek or giving her a hug. For reasons unknown to me I loved the little blond girl best of all the children in the home.

A maid popped her head around the door. "Sit down girls and be quiet," she said. We did for a while and then we were up and at it again.

"Let's go in the other playroom," Ann said. We stood in the doorway for a moment, then slowly wheedled our way into the

13

room. No one noticed us as we observed grown up relatives cuddling their children, sitting them on their laps and talking with them. I crept closer and watched in fascination as a grandpa in uniform showed his two grandsons his right thumb, swinging it around like a rag doll—the middle part had no bone. Suddenly he looked up and saw me.

"Go away nigger," he said, "We don't want niggers around here." I backed away—wandered into the hallway and sat down dejectedly on one of the boxes. I stared at the floor and wondered what a nigger might be? *Something nasty,* I supposed, because that man didn't like me. I hastily brushed away a tear, jumped up and ran into the other playroom where Hazil, as soon as she saw me, stretched out her arms saying, "Mare-wee, Mare-wee." I hugged her hard and kissed her cheek.

Soon the relatives said their last good-byes and some of them cried. Sister St. Claire instructed us children to go and stand by certain maids or nuns. We divided into groups of five or so and then went to Mr. Cattermole's fleet of cars parked in the laneway. I followed the maids, Bertha and Sheila, plus their two little girls about the same age as me. They were wives of husbands serving in the forces. Reverend Mother had given them board and lodging along with their children, in exchange for their services. "Stay close," Bertha said, and I traipsed behind obediently. The car's interior had two plush seats facing each other and single flat pull-down ones on each side. The two maids took a seat each and arranged themselves, their daughters, purses, and lunch boxes.

"You sit there, Mary," said Bertha, pointing to one of the pull-down seats.

As our car pulled away from the curb, I pressed my nose to the window and saw Reverend Mother blowing kisses at me.

We had been driving for a long time and my eyes kept closing. My head wouldn't stay put, even when I rested it against the window. The car came to a halt on a side road and we clambered out to pee behind bushes. Then we got back into the car to eat a lunch of corned beef sandwiches and rice pudding–rice pudding that had been baked in the oven and had a brown slimy skin over it.

"I don't like this," whined Sally, Bertha's little girl.

Bertha took her spoon, scooped it up, and plunked it on my plate, saying, "Let Mary have it." I didn't like it either and I immediately threw up all over myself and onto Bertha who ordered me out of the car where she cleaned me up, all the while telling me I was an ungrateful child. As I climbed back into the car, our driver, Mr. Cattermole's brother, gave me a wink. He didn't talk much, but he did say to me, "We'll soon be there, Mary."

"Mary smells," complained Sally as we drove on. I just stared out of the window and curbed my excitement at seeing cows and sheep and the sea in the distance, just as Reverend Mother had said.

As the cars wended their way higher and higher into Torquay's hilly terrain, the road finally leveled out and around mid-afternoon, the cars pulled into a sloping driveway to stop in front of Lyncourt, a large gray house with purple gables.

"That's the sea," I heard Ann saying as she exited from the car in front.

I ran to her side and stared in wonder at millions of lights dancing on its surface. My childish mind could not articulate what I felt. My senses took in the fresh air mingled with the smell of the sea. And I loved it.

Sister Maria, who always spoke quietly and for most of the time had a worried look, had been at our new home called Lyncourt for a few days. Other staff had come under her supervision as she organized and prepared for our arrival. "Mary and Ann, come on in. You as well," she called to two of the boys.

The drivers and staff carried trunks, cases and bags into the foyer. They put the baggage down on the black and white checkered tiles. "Go to the room at the end," Sister Maria said, in her soft voice. Not everyone heard her, so Elsie, our cook, shouted, "Oi children, follow me." She moved at a quick pace and we followed eagerly along the carpeted passageway and into a huge room with parquet flooring and wide bay windows.

There were rows of mattresses on the floor made ready for sleeping. Some of us ran to peer out of the windows and look at the sea again. Outside a stone balcony ran the length of the house; its stone ornamental pillars positioned so closely together gave it a safe, solid look.

"Aw right then sit down in a row right 'ere," Elsie said, indicating the polished floor along by the big bay windows. Laughing and tumbling over each other we obeyed. Elsie was like Nellie, the cook, who stayed back in London. I just knew she loved us. She was fat and jolly with eyes as blue as the sea.

"Mary smells," Sally announced.

"I 'spect we all do after that long drive," said Elsie, which set us laughing all the more. We quieted down as Sister St. Claire and Sister Maria came into the room.

"Girls, you will sleep in here," said Sister St. Claire, "but first of all go with Sister Faith and Elsie—you're going to have baths before supper. Boys, you follow Sister Maria and Dolly." With some pushing for first place, the boys scooted over to Sister Maria where she encouraged them to get in line and follow her.

The newness of our surroundings excited us. We were about six girls and five "little ones," as the toddlers were called. I held onto Hazil. "Up Mare-wee, up," she said, as we clambered up a grand stairway with a wooden banister of ornate design. We peered into large airy rooms as we followed Elsie. Sister Faith brought up the rear and directed us to go into a room close to the bathroom. One of the maids came huffing and puffing up the stairs carrying suitcases marked "Girls' Clothing." She helped Sister Faith sort the garments into piles, while Elsie organized the baths.

"Come on Ann and Mary, let's start with you," she said. We had to step on a stool to get into the tub with its claw feet. The water, warm and welcoming, soothed us. With Elsie's encouragement we soaped ourselves. She washed our hair using coal tar soap and when we were done, Sister Faith, who must have been the gentlest creature that ever lived, rubbed us dry.

"There," she said, "how does that feel?" She gave us clean clothes, long vests, and baggy knickers that tended to sag on our thin bodies. Then from a pile of dresses we picked out ones that fitted. We helped with the younger ones as the baths progressed. Happy busyness prevailed.

After baths and tea the nuns took us for a walk around the grounds. At the side of the house a stretch of lawn swept down in a gentle slope to winding pathways. An abundance of shrubs and foliage filled the flowerbeds and wherever we looked—the sea surrounded us.

A man pushing a wheelbarrow stopped and touched his cap. The sisters acknowledged him with smiles and we moved on. I turned to look at the man. He remained there eyeing us intently through his thick-lensed glasses.

5

They Find us Again

September 1941:

A few months later, with ever-increasing raids on London, Reverend Mother sent some of the nursing home patients to Torquay where they became the occupants of the large airy rooms of Lyncourt. This necessitated us, the children, being moved into a cottage on the grounds. The cottage had five small rooms upstairs, a tiny bathroom, and one toilet, plus an outhouse. Sister St. Claire lived with us in the cottage and became our main caregiver.

Attached to the cottage, a large barn had been converted into a chapel and every day of the week before breakfast we went in there to pray. And every day of the week we trudged to Torwood Primary School for classes.

On Sunday mornings we walked to St. Michael's and All Angel's Church for services. I loved singing the hymns and listening to the kind father who conducted the services. He paid attention to us children and always had us go to the front of the church while he spoke directly to us.

"Now children," he would say, "sometimes it might seem that God doesn't care about you anymore, because of the bombs and the bad things that happen to people we know and maybe even to you. But He's watching and He loves you. Even though it is hard for you, there are children in other parts of the world who are affected by the war—some who are a lot worse off than you." He told us about those other children in faraway places and about the little brown children in Africa, which so resonated with me that I sang with great fervor, along with the other children, a hymn that always brought a lump to my throat:

> Over the sea there are little brown children,
>   fathers and mothers and babies dear,
> They have not heard of the dear Lord Jesus
>   no one has told them that God is near,
> Swift let the message go over the water,
>   telling the children that God is near.
> Little brown children the teachers are coming,
>   speeding to love you and help and cheer
> Soon you will hear of the dear Lord Jesus,
>   soon they will tell you that God is near
> Swift let the message go over the water
>   telling the children that God is near.

(Anonymous)

I always hoped someone would go.

When we arrived back at the cottage after service we had dinner, then with folded arms we rested our heads on the table. It was a time to think—to dream, and to wonder. Wonder when I'd see my Reverend Mother again. After rest we went for a walk or read Bible stories and other books, like the Enid Blyton adventure stories for children and Wind in the Willows and Milly Molly Mandy. I loved books and very often had one hidden under my mattress for times when I was sent to bed early as punishment.

On Sunday evenings at precisely 6:00 p.m., we walked from the cottage along an unpaved driveway, past Gardener Grimshaw's woodshed, past the strawberry patch and into Lyncourt for vespers, an evening service. Teatime—our last meal of the day—had been eaten at 4:30 p.m. and consisted of one and a half slices of bread with margarine, half a jam or honey sandwich, and a Peek Frean biscuit with a cup of milk. Sister St. Claire had a pot of tea and her own plate of bread and butter and sometimes cake.

Once in the large bedded ward, we politely went around saying good evening to the ladies in their high hospital beds. "It's just plain good manners," Sister St. Claire would say.

One of the old ladies, Miss Pierce, who doused herself with liberal quantities of Yardley's lavender water, always asked us if we were being good at school and we dutifully replied that we were. Maids pushed patients in their beds from the smaller wards and chairs were arranged in the center for the nuns and staff and we sat in rows on the floor. Sister St. Claire conducted the service. We always said the same prayers and repeated part of Psalm 91 in a sing-song fashion:

He that dwelleth in the secret place of the most High shall abide under the shadow of the Almighty... Surely He shall deliver thee from the snare of the fowler, and from the noisome pestilence... Thou shalt not be afraid of the terror by night; nor for the arrow that flyeth by day... A thousand shall fall at thy side... but it shall not come nigh thee...

But that wasn't totally true; terror plagued us again, and worse than arrows—terror came in fighter planes and bombs. Somehow the Germans found out where we were and once more at nighttime we were running for cover, scrambling down the narrow wooden stairs of the cottage and into the steel structured Morrison shelters set up in the playroom. The shelters served as dining tables too, which meant we were either sitting around them or diving under them when the raids happened. The shelters looked like steel cages and had solid flat tops and spring floors that were covered with thick felt. Room was sparse and we had to huddle together. It was even harder for Sister St. Claire—she had to lay sideways. And there we'd stay, listening to the steady drone of the planes as they made their way up the coast to London, dropping bombs as they went. Sister had us sing songs while we were there. "Sing up," she'd say. We really didn't feel like singing, but we did our best.

The adults talked about the war all the time. One particular piece of news filled me with terror; a German submarine had been caught in the harbor. And then one Saturday afternoon a few days later, a plane flew low and shot people as they lay sunbathing on the beach. Then—horror of horrors—the next week as we were playing on the lawn, running after each other in a game of "butterfly-chase," Mr. Morgan, the warden, jumped up from his deck chair.

"Get inside," he screamed, "Hurry! Hurry!" I heard the familiar drone of the plane and almost before we started running it was there, flying so low I could see the pilot. I grabbed Hazil's hand and we could hear the machine gun fire as we raced, screaming up the side path, across the driveway and into the house, where we stood shaking with fear and something akin to anger as the plane receded. I instinctively cuddled Hazil, my inseparable little friend, and we stood together crying and trembling.

Elsie, Sister Faith, and others calmed us with kind murmurings and hugs. "Hush, hush my dears," said Sister Faith, as she stroked our heads. "It'll be alright." And dear Elsie, lifting her voice asked, "Aw right then, 'oo wants some 'ot chocolate then?" The sobbing quieted. I wiped my eyes with the back of my hand and looked at Elsie, as we all did. "This way my darlin's," she said. And happily we followed her along the hallway and down the stairs to the maids' sitting room where we huddled together in the big sofas and armchairs.

Sister Faith and Dolly, Elsie's kitchen maid, went to make hot chocolate for us. And when they were gone Elsie said, "Oo wants to 'ear the story of the Reverend then?" The Reverend was the resident priest, who lived in a small apartment in the priory in Thames Ditton. We'd heard the story before and we started to giggle. "Now quiet," she said, "or I won't tell ya."

Elsie lowered her voice and spoke slowly. "It was like this then, back in Thames Ditton, the Reverend tried to make a short cut to the shelter when the siren went off. So what did 'ee do, 'ee tried to get hisself through the serving 'atch from the kitchen into the refectory. But 'is tummy was so big it got in the way. So," she said, opening her eyes wide and rolling them around, "someone 'ad to push and someone 'ad to pull, an' all the while they was doin' that, the Reverend got redder and redder and very cross. Then suddenly plop!" Elsie banged on the sideboard, "'ee lands wiv a thump on the polished floor." No matter how many times Elsie told us this tale the response was the same and we were laughing so hard by the time the hot chocolate arrived that the raid was almost forgotten.

But the raids and the stories we heard about other people's experiences played over and over in my mind and I started to have nightmares. Night after night the same one occurred; monsters came to the end of my bed and chanted, "We're going to take you to Germany." These ghastly apparitions pushed my bed slowly out of the room and I lay there petrified. Eventually I'd wake up soaking wet.

My continued bed-wetting was my nemesis. Every child exhibited some odd behavior as a way of coping, such as thumb and finger sucking, hair chewing and nail biting, banging heads against the wall and rocking back and forth with knees clutched to the chest. The bed-wetting was the worst of these behaviors, and seen as extreme naughtiness. Punishment for this offence continued unabated. Sister St. Claire spanked us, sent us to bed without tea, our last meal of the day, made us stand in a corner for long periods, or banished us to solitary confinement in the coal cupboard—one of the worst punishments for me—all implemented to try and make us better behaved. In the coal cupboard I imagined every monster possible rising from the black coal. And the worst of it was that Sister St. Claire often forgot that I or one of the other children were there. The children who bit their nails and sucked various fingers periodically had their hands dipped in a solution of bitter aloes, the taste so foul they couldn't resort to their comforting behavior for quite awhile.

Without a doubt I was the worst of the bed-wetters. Not a night went by but I'd wake up wet. I tried to stay awake until the sirens went off or until after we had been in the shelter, but all to no avail. Each morning came bringing the same results. I don't think Sister knew how hard I tried to contain myself or realized how thrilled I'd be to tell her one morning that I had woken up dry. Instead, each morning I would wait to learn what my punishment would be.

One day Sister told me that discussions had ensued between her and the headmistress of Torwood School and they had agreed that the only way to stop my bed-wetting was to inform my classmates of my sin. Shattered, I tried to fight back tears as I waited outside the headmistress' office. There were three people in there, Sister, the headmistress, and my teacher, Miss Hockings, who was being informed of the new regimen. When Miss Hockings came out her eyes were red and puffy.

"Come with me Mary," she said, in a small voice. She held my hand and gave it a squeeze. In the classroom she told me to sit at my desk. My schoolmates were already seated. She explained to the class that every morning I would have to let her know whether I wet my bed or not. An audible gasp was heard. Children looked at me and snickered. "Be quiet and listen," she said. She sounded angry and I didn't understand why. I knew I was her favorite pupil. Miss Hockings held up a chart with my name at the top. Empty squares waited for the check marks that I knew would go into them.

At the end of the lesson out in the corridor children teased and mocked me. It was all too much for my crushed soul; the pent up tears escaped, accompanied by a loud cry of anguish, and I ran back into the classroom to Miss Hockings. She sat at her desk marking papers. She looked up and then held out her arms for me to take solace and comfort in her loving embrace. She stroked my curls and rocked me, murmuring kind words and told me we probably wouldn't have the chart for long. But she comforted me the most by telling me she knew I couldn't help wetting the bed. "And," she said giving me a squeeze, "don't forget you're the best reader in my class!"

My troubles made me think of my friend John; he also couldn't help the way he behaved. His mum got killed in one of the air raids and his dad was fighting overseas. He lived with Mrs. Bishop and her daughter, Kathleen, who happened to be my best friend at school. I was often invited to the Bishops for tea and met John there when we were both eight.

"Do you want to play Snakes and Ladders?" he asked on our first encounter. I looked at the warmth in his dark eyes and I nodded. "Come on then," he said, sitting up to the table and opening the box. A little nervous, I hesitated for a moment then sat on the chair beside him. We played and John laughed when I beat him, saying, "I'll win the next one." I liked John and the way he laughed. And I liked the way he always talked to me when I went to Mrs. Bishop's house.

On Kathleen's eighth birthday, I and five other children were at the house for her party. Cookies, cake, and Jell-O were a treat during the war and we ate with relish. Afterwards we played "blind man's bluff." Mrs. Bishop tied a scarf around John's eyes, because he wanted to play the "catcher." She spun him round three times and then we hid behind furniture and squealed each time John's outstretched arms came close.

"I'm coming to get you," he chanted. Suddenly he stopped, and struggled to pull off the scarf. "Let me tell you about my mum," he said, "she was just taking our supper out of the oven when—boom." He made explosive noises through his lips and continued, "Her head went one way and her arm blew off."

"John stop!" said Mrs. Bishop. She told us not to take any notice and suggested we play "I spy." "Find a place to sit children," she urged.

I sat on the settee. John came and sat next to me and I was glad. Sometimes our friends said in a sing-song manner, "John likes Mary and Mary likes John." And I'd giggle and say, "No I don't." But really I did.

6

Gas Masks, Tripe and Miss Angel

We never did like the gas masks, but Sister St. Claire said we had to carry them at all times. They had to be placed by our beds at night and we hung them, in their cardboard boxes, around our necks when we went to school. If an adult told us to put them on we had to obey immediately; otherwise we could die, we were told. One warm Saturday morning we were into our usual practice of gas mask drill, feeling overcome by the horrible rubbery smell. But nevertheless we held hands in a big circle in the yard outside the cottage. With the empty square cardboard boxes hanging around our necks swinging back and forth, we traipsed around and around trying to sing *Here We Go Round the Mulberry Bush*. But the masks steamed up and our voices were muffled.

"You can take them off now," said Sister. With relief we removed the masks. I stood next to Alan, a boy about my own age. We concentrated on pushing our gas masks into our boxes and helping the little ones do the same with their Mickey Mouse and Donald Duck masks. And as always, I helped Hazil.

"Oh no; look who's coming." Alan said under his breath. I looked up to see the familiar figure of Miss Angel, limping up the driveway toward us. She usually showed up once a week offering to help.

"How are you my dear?" Sister St. Claire asked.

Miss Angel responded with a toothless grin, "I'm fine Sister." Even though the day was hot she wore a brown winter coat buttoned up to the neck—the only clothing we ever saw her in, which caused an unpleasant odor to emanate from her.

She was one of many people who volunteered to help but when Miss Angel came, Sister St. Claire would say, "There's nothing to do really. Why don't you just rest for a while?"

The old lady always sat in a chair in the playroom and talked. "The war is terrible," she'd say. "Hitler will be punished one of these days." Then she'd stare ahead lost in her own world, wiping beads of sweat off her face with a gray handkerchief.

This time Sister St. Claire found something for Miss Angel to do. "The maids will be bringing the dinner soon," she said. "Could you supervise the boys? They can go to the outhouse before we eat."

"Shall I take your coat for you Miss Angel?" Alan asked with an angelic smile.

"Be quiet Alan," Sister said. She glared at the rest of us as we tried to muffle our giggles. "Dinner will be here soon. Off you go. Brian, you lead the way," she said to one of the older boys.

"Come on, little fellows. I'll keep an eye on you," said Miss Angel.

We girls went to the upstairs toilet to freshen up for dinner. And soon we were all seated on wooden benches around the two Morrison shelters.

Ada, the maid from Thames Ditton, had come to Torquay and now assisted Elsie in the kitchen. Meals for everyone were prepared in the big house and maids brought the food to the cottage. Ada came into the cottage and placed a large pot on the small serving table "It's tripe today Sister," she said. Another maid came close behind with a pot of powdered mashed potatoes. My stomach churned. I knew that I and half of the children would be struggling to eat dinner that day. Miss Angel sat on a chair at the end of the serving table passing plates to Sister St. Claire, who carefully ladled the tripe and potatoes onto the plates, handing them to Alan and Ann to place in front of us.

Tripe had a tough, rubbery texture to it and knowing we were eating the lining of cow's stomach didn't help. No amount of onion sauce made with powdered milk could take away its awful taste. I knew I would not be having bread and butter for tea, but be struggling to down the rest of the tripe when teatime came. Sister had a rule that any food left on our plates had to be eaten up at the next meal.

"Mary."

"Yes Sister." I emerged from my reverie.

"Eat up, and you, Alan! Brian! We haven't got all day."

Most of the children had finished the meal but I and three others stood before Sister with our plates. "Get the covers, you know where to put them," she said. And dutifully we placed them in the cupboard in the corner of the room.

With dinner over at least for some, the same two children who had handed out the dishes would be responsible to wash the plates. Two of the older boys filled jugs with hot water from the bathroom, brought them down to the playroom and poured the water into an enamel bowl for washing.

In an hour or so, Ada returned for the pots. "Did everyone finish their meal Sister?" she asked, with her green eyes fixed on me.

"No—the ingratitude for all we do, it's sometimes hard to understand. To think I've given my life to look after you children." Sister glared at those of us who had failed to finish our meals.

Ada picked up the pots. "Sister," she said, "would you like me to come and help you with the children's baths this evening? I know washing so many heads of hair is a big job."

"Oh, no dear, you take your time off."

But Ada smiling, and with perceived goodwill, insisted. She didn't mind at all, she said.

7

Bath Night

I was seven, maybe eight, when Ada offered to help Sister on hair washing nights. Her assaults started gradually. At first she held me under the water for a second or two, but slowly her attacks became more vicious. The abuse happened on Saturdays. Saturday evenings loomed dark and sinister in my mind.

"Cleanliness is next to godliness," Sister St. Claire told us many times, "and you must be clean and scrubbed for the Lord's Day." That's why hair washing was a part of the Saturday night routine. And for those of us who wet the bed we had another quick, but cold bath in the morning because the fire had not been lit in the playroom and the fire heated the water in the tank.

"I'm ready for the next one Sister," Ada called down the stairs. A few of us remained in the playroom reading books. With each announcement from Doris, my stomach churned. Sister looked up from her reading.

"Up you go Mary." Reluctantly, I went up the stairs and slowly made my way along the narrow passageway to the bathroom.

Ada stood in the bathroom doorway impatiently tapping her foot. "Hurry up Mary, for goodness sake," she snapped. I slid past her and started to undress. I stood there naked, my thin body shivering in spite of the steam and heat.

"Get in then." Ada stood, hands on hips, giving the order. The sharp command again made my stomach churn. I hesitated at the side of the old tub in the tiny bathroom. Above me, the skylight loomed as disturbing as the foreboding presence in the room. Nothing covered it and beyond was the sheer blackness of night.

"Please don't do it." I pleaded. "You promised not to do it anymore." I looked at my tormentor.

"Shut up and do as you're told," she said. "You should be grateful that there's water to have a bath. Do you know how many children in this war haven't seen a bathroom for months and have nobody to look after them?"

"Yes Ada," I said, although I didn't know and I didn't care. I only cared about me at that moment. My mouth was dry and my stomach in tight knots. The knots hurt.

I looked at Ada's small, green eyes with the hard black core in the center of each, the long sallow face and the square jaw. I saw the largeness of her, and the rough square hands that soon would inflict their weekly torture. I tried again to plead my case.

"You did promise after last week that you wouldn't do it again."

"Did I now?" There was a suggestion that she might relent. I looked up quickly.

"Yes," I said, hope rising. "Don't you remember? I couldn't breathe for a long time."

"That's an exaggeration, you were just play acting. You don't want to have your hair washed. That's it plain and simple, isn't it?" I remained silent. Ada continued, "If you hadn't had a black father, you wouldn't have thick black curls and it wouldn't take so long to wash."

I felt a lump in my throat that somehow went with the ache behind my eyes. That meant tears might flow, which would only make her hurt me more. So I determined I wouldn't cry. But I couldn't do anything about my dry mouth, churning stomach and tight chest.

"In you get." The order brought me back to the moment and panic jumped to the fore. I could hear the beat of my heart pounding in my ears.

I spoke again. My voice sounded distant. "Please don't, Ada," I begged, "please," while stepping into the deep, soapy, dirty bath water that several children had bathed in already. I resigned myself to the moment, but at the same time hoped that Ada might reconsider. I sat down and reached for the washcloth and wiped my face with trembling hands.

She stood watching me. "You don't need to do that," she snapped. "I'll be washing your face." I rubbed my body in spasmodic movement. She said, "All right, I won't do it tonight." I looked up, not sure whether to say anything. I attempted a smile, but my mouth wouldn't cooperate, just too dry. "Lie down then. Let's get your hair wet." I gripped the sides of the tub and lay down. Ada leaned over the tub swishing the water through my hair. She curtly ordered me to sit up. I sensed her anger. She rubbed the coal tar soap into my hair and I could feel her fingers hard on my scalp, massaging until it hurt. A thick lather covered my head. Suddenly with lightning speed her large soapy hands were all over my face. I cried out, shutting my eyes quickly and groping for the washcloth, but I couldn't find it. I cupped water into my hands in an effort to rinse the soap from my eyes. Then I stood up.

"Can I have a towel Ada? My eyes hurt."

"No you cannot. I have to rinse the soap off first. Sit down." But I had to know. I had to see her. I could tell by her expression if she was going to do it or not.

"Please don't; you promised." I looked at Ada through my stinging eyes, but she refused eye contact. The knot got tighter in my stomach.

"Yes, I did promise, now lie down." I sat down slowly and then lay down. I watched her watching me. I saw the hatred in her eyes and I knew. I gulped in air as best as I could as Ada's strong hand came down on my forehead. In my panic I had difficulty in remembering to keep my mouth closed—the tendency being to yell out. Dirty water flowed into my mouth, nostrils, and ears. With an iron grip, she held me down. I struggled frantically; the swirling blackness and the crushing sensation in my chest increased my efforts to break free. Just as suddenly, Ada let go. As I emerged, I heard her laughing.

Gasping, coughing, spluttering, my body trembling, I struggled up. "You promised, *you promised*," I sobbed.

8

The Storm

We lived high up in the hills of Torquay. Going to school was easy, downhill all the way. We went at a fair pace, anxious to get inside in case of a raid. We knew we were not to pick up anything in the gutter—it could be shrapnel or something that might blow us to pieces. Every day, Sister and the teachers reminded us of this fact. Our day at school always started with the Lord's Prayer and hymn sing. We sang hymns asking God to take care of those in peril on the sea and hymns thanking Him for our protection.

My mothering instinct always led me to take charge at the end of the school day and I stood near the exit waiting for the Lyncourt "home children," as we were called, to come from their classes.

On one occasion Miss Tiffany, one of the teachers, who we had nicknamed the dragon lady because of her constant anger, came down the passageway firmly holding Alan's arm. Her high heels clicked as she walked. Her heavy makeup, bright red lipstick, and carefully groomed hair were still in place even at the end of the school day. Through clenched teeth she growled, "You are a dreadful child and I will see to it that you're punished." Alan clamped his mouth shut in a defiant manner and tried to escape her hold.

"What's going on here?" Miss Spurr, the headmistress, came quickly toward us.

Miss Tiffany released Alan. Her face redder than usual, she started to explain Alan's misdemeanor, but Miss Spurr interrupted. "We'll deal with this tomorrow," she said. "The children need to get home. It looks like rain." But we knew she wouldn't deal with it tomorrow. There were too many other issues, like the endless instructions about what to do in an air attack, the practice sessions with our gas masks, and diving under the desks at the count of three. We liked Miss Spurr, even though her front teeth stuck out like a row of tombstones and she didn't have a much of a chin. And I liked her even more because she had told sister the bed-wetting chart could not be maintained by the school anymore.

"Well, Mary," she said, "is everyone here?" I glanced around and counted each familiar face—two were missing. Within seconds Bobby and Ann arrived, disheveled and panting.

Soon we were out on the narrow pavement. We lined up in twos, and started stamping our feet. "One, two, three, go," I shouted. We swung into the familiar rhythm, away from the school and up the incline toward home. Clop! Clop! Clop! Clop! We grinned as our shoes struck the pavement in perfect unison. Our wartime shoes were of a poor quality and soles with holes—a common occurrence. Gardener Grimshaw hammered blakeys in our shoes to prevent the soles wearing out so quickly. The half-moon shaped reinforcers made a sharp staccato sound as we stomped our feet. And we reveled in that sound as the echoes bounced off the stone walled cottages. We climbed higher and higher into the hilly terrain of Torquay and far below us the seawaters slapped against the harbor wall.

A low rumbling in the distance and the oppressive air told us a thunderstorm brewed in our vicinity. We heard another rumble, louder this time. Bobby stopped. "I think it's a raid," he said squinting up at the sky through his thick-lensed glasses. We faltered in our marching. Fear was etched in the faces around me and I heard my own heartbeat strumming in my ears.

"It's just thunder," Alan said, "let's run to the high wall before the rain starts." A loud crack of thunder and large raindrops splashed all around us as we ran. The wind teased the treetops, coaxing them this way and that and then descended in giant sweeps, tugging rudely at our thin summer clothing. Lightning added to the mix.

High up the barrage balloons did an elephant dance. They dotted the sky acting as a deterrent to the Luftwaffe to prevent low flying attacks. The balloons were attached to metal cables and we knew that enemy planes avoided getting entangled in them. We ran harder and as we did, Hazil tripped and fell. I bent down to help her, then stopped in my tracks as she let out a blood-curdling scream. Following her terrified upward gaze to see a fireball careening toward us, I pulled her to her feet, held her hand tightly and yelled, "Run, Hazil, run!" We reached the wall and stood panting, with our backs pressed against it staring up at the ball of fire. "It's one of the balloons. It's been hit by the lightening," Alan said. We watched the flames licking greedily around the gray metal structure. But then the fire dwindled and the skeletal remains just floated away. The storm's growling softened, the lightening lessened, and the sun made a decided effort to pierce the dark clouds.

"I told you so," said Alan with exaggerated smugness. We started laughing almost hysterically. "Let's go," I shouted and we swung into our march again. We didn't care that our paper-thin shoes squelched with the noise of the water or that the staccato sound of our blakeys was now muffled as we went.

9

Peaches

"Come on in then."

I hesitated as I stood in the doorway of Gardener Grimshaw's woodshed, basket in hand. "Sister sent me for the peaches" I said. He took the basket from me.

"Come on in then," he said again. He put his big hand on my shoulder and steered me to the back of the shed. Smells of earth and wood invaded my nostrils. I liked the smell; it made me think of the outdoors. Narrow shelves were stacked with cans, garden tools, and paintbrushes. I had to step carefully; it was dark after the bright sunlight. The trees and bushes that grew all around the shed didn't allow much light in through the narrow windows.

He placed the basket on the workbench. That meant he planned to do it to me again, because the peaches were in the greenhouse across the pathway from the shed. Gardener Grimshaw sat down on his bench, leaned over to the ledge and held up a large peach. I smiled a little nervously.

"Would you like it?" he said. I nodded. He grinned and reached for me with his free hand. He wrapped his arm around my waist and lifted me on to his lap. "Eat up," he said, giving me the peach. I bit into it and the juice ran down my chin. He chuckled and mopped it up with his large white hanky, then he gave me a hug pulling me closer. I smelled tobacco on the bib of his dungarees. He started to nibble at my ear and whispered, "We won't tell anyone, will we?" I shook my head and took another bite of the peach. He poked his tongue into my ear and I shuddered. "You like peaches don't you?" I nodded.

His warm hand rested on my skinny thigh and moved up slowly, squeezing gently...

10

The Coming of the Americans

In January 1942, the first American forces started arriving in England. Sister had told us about the Americans and that they were our friends. On our way home from school one day we heard a rumbling sound coming from the main road that cut through the town center. Our marching stopped, and we looked and waited.

"What is it?" Bobby asked.

"I hope it's not the Germans," Alan intoned.

Fear gripped me once more. I remembered my recurring dream. *We're coming to take you to Germany.* Soon an enormous tank came into view. We stood frozen, staring, but as it came closer we saw the American flag and the smiling faces of soldiers waving at us. Another one followed close behind and another. We watched fascinated as twenty-four of these huge amphibious tanks wound their way up the incline. We jumped up and down, shouting and waving, and the Americans responded with waves and greetings.

"Look at the size of them," Bobby said excitedly.

"They're going to beat Hitler," Alan said, as he jumped up and down. We had to wait until they'd all passed before we could cross the road toward home.

We were almost home when we saw Sister in the distance. We started to run toward her and a dozen different voices tried to explain our tardiness. "One at a time children! Mary, tell me what you saw."

"We counted twenty-four of them, Sister."

"Twenty-four what, Mary?" she asked with a smile. Her smile was a blessing. I knew she understood our enthusiasm. The rest of the day and all through teatime, when usually no talking was permitted, we talked about those tanks!

A week later on our way home from school, three American soldiers were strolling toward us on the other side of the road.

We stopped and they stopped. Crossing the road they came toward us. "Hi kids. How ya doin'?"

Alan said, "We're going home."

Two of them were black and suddenly they seemed to notice me. They both stared and I backed away. "Don't be frightened honey," one of them said. I can't recall how it happened but they walked along with us to Lyncourt, and so began an extraordinary relationship with these kindhearted, carefree people—their demeanor and culture so different from our own. They came often and played chase with us in the garden, swung us around and wrestled with the boys. We loved them. They were our American friends.

Sometime later we were out for a walk on a Sunday afternoon with our new puppy, "Scruffy." Reverend Mother's Airedale dog in Thames Ditton had given birth to puppies and Sister had been up to the Home of Compassion to bring one of the pups back for us. We believed she had picked out the best one of the litter.

"Heel, Scruffy," Sister St. Claire commanded, but our puppy didn't understand and strained at the leash that Sister held. Our delight at the little dog became diverted as the biggest car we had ever seen drove past us. We gaped as the car stopped, reversed and glided to a standstill beside us.

"Hello Sister. Would the kids like a ride?" asked the American driver.

"Well thank you," she said. He stepped briskly out of his car and opened the doors in no time.

"Hop in kids," he said, with a wide grin. But we couldn't just hop in—that wasn't the way we were taught; we looked at Sister and waited to be told to "hop in." Sister started naming names, but not mine. *Oh, please God make Sister say mine.* About fifteen packed into that car and the rest of us still stood on the pavement until she had finished. Our cheerful American whisked around to the drivers seat. "Okay kids," he said looking at us, "your turn when we get back." We waited on the pavement with Scruffy and waved as this cheerful character pulled away telling us he'd be back in ten minutes. When my turn came I offered a silent thank you to God as I sped away, sandwiched between Shirley and Ann and squealing with delight as we roared through the usually quiet Lincombe roads.

11

Overcrowded

Through 1943 and 1944, Reverend Mother continued to send more children down from Thames Ditton to live in the cottage, children whose relatives had begged her for help. Approximately 30 children squeezed together for meals around the two Morrison shelters, sometimes getting into squabbles because of our close proximity.

Sister always had us sit in the same spot. Mine happened to be close to the wall and this gave me a way to discard the food that turned my stomach—like gristly beef, tripe, and the fat out of the corned beef. I pushed it off my plate onto the Morrison table, and then at a convenient moment stealthily slid it to the wall where it fell and remained held securely in place by the criss-cross wire side of the shelter. My deed did not remain a secret for long. The smell had come to Sister's attention and Ada did a successful nose search.

"Do you realize," Sister St. Claire said, as I stood before her, "do you realize how fortunate you are to have food on your plate?" I hung my head, because I couldn't think of anything to say.

And that is how it was that from then on I had to sit close to Sister. My short respite from eating the foods I hated—gone! Now the foods I had not been able to swallow were placed in front of me for each meal in succession, so portions of cold, gristly beef would be my lot for breakfast, lunch, and dinner.

Upstairs we were crowded with smaller children sleeping two in a bed, but in the summer evenings when the heat filled the cottage and Sister went over to the big house to spend time with the other nuns, we played rather than staying in bed. Our favorite game, "Feet Off Ground," had us jumping from bed to bed and room to room. Broken bedsprings were always a problem. Gardener Grimshaw supplied Sister with planks of wood, which were placed between the mattress and what was left of the springs. We took turns watching for Sister's return and with much giggling and scrambling, we toppled into our beds before she entered the cottage.

Big felt curtains hung in all the windows and each evening Mr. Morgan stood in the yard looking up to see that no chinks of light peeped through. "We don't want the bombers to know where we are," he'd say. "Make sure you listen carefully." And one of us took instruction as he had us pull the curtains into place.

Life continued and our daily routines were predictable until one day in the summer of 1944 when Sister told us as we sat around the table that some of us would be going away. "The cottage is too crowded," she said. "Some of you will go to nice people in their private homes, just until the war is over." Then she told us who would be going.

A day or two later, staff chatted in the crowded playroom with people we didn't know. Ten children sat on a bench with glum expressions. Ada busied herself giving each child a carrier bag of clothing. Sister studied a list she held in her hand. She looked up. "Judy, you're going with Mrs. Lawson."

A short woman with a pleasant round face stepped forward as nine-year-old Judy stood up. "Come along dear," she said. And away they went. This miserable situation continued as these strangers went away with our playmates. Twenty of us remained.

Tears splashed down my face as a big man took Hazil's hand and she, trembling and sobbing, clutched a worn out teddy bear and stretched her other hand out toward me. But away the big man took her and his timid little wife followed behind with Hazil's bag.

Gloom pervaded my heart that day and I cried myself to sleep.

12

It's Over

May 8, 1945:

Three months shy of my eleventh birthday on a glorious day in May 1945, we learned the war had ended. I remember the elation as we ran home from school—shouting and laughing and chanting derogatory rhymes about Hitler. No more shelters and gas masks. Hurrah. The town buzzed with activity. Reverend Mother came, and what joy to see her again.

All the children returned to the cottage for a while and eventually some went back to their families. But on that first day, the foster parents stood chatting with each other and the children remained by them—hesitant until Sister encouraged them to come and play with us. I wanted to take Hazil. But she sat on that big man's knee, looking lost and frightened.

"Shall I take Hazil?" I asked Sister, and she nodded.

"Come on Hazil. Do you want to play?" I said, slipping into my mothering role. She stood there making no response and her face puckered up close to tears. I took her hand and led her to the play area. For a while, I worked at coaxing her to play. She seemed fearful of everything and I felt anger toward that man who had just brought her back. My childish mind believed he had done bad things to her.

I tried again. "Do you want to play 'mothers and fathers?'" I said. "Would you like that Hazil?" I bent down, willing her to look at me. "Mothers and fathers" was one of our favorite games. I said to Alan, "You play father and I'll be mother." Using cardboard boxes to create walls and some boxes as tables we entered our make-believe world of families. Pouring make-believe tea from enamel toy teapots with Walt Disney characters painted on them, I handed a cup to Hazil. "Now you drink that." She carefully took the little cup and smiled. We were back together again.

Gifts of clothing came from South Africa. I can still see the bright blue dresses with orange flowers and butterflies all over them and the pink cardigans with marble shaped buttons. The packages included shirts, plus fours, and pullovers for the boys. Dressed up in our new finery we headed to town in char-à-bancs, accompanied by Reverend Mother, Sister, other nuns, and maids. What exhilaration we experienced riding in the huge sightseeing buses with their red plush seats.

Victory parties abounded and children by the hundreds, including us, poured into town halls and clubs to eat red, white and blue iced cake; we wore red, white and blue party hats and sang patriotic songs with great gusto, among them, *"There'll Always be an England."* "Come on everyone," shouted the emcee, as he hoisted his accordion and come on we did! He sang the verse and we all joined in the chorus singing at the top of our voices:

There'll always be an England,
While there's a country lane,
Wherever there's a cottage small
Beside a field of grain.

There'll always be an England,
While there's a busy street,
Wherever there's a turning wheel,
A million marching feet.

Red, white and blue,
What does it mean to you?
Surely you're proud
Shout it aloud.

Britons awake! The Empire too,
We can depend on you,
Freedom remains
These are the chains
Nothing can break.
There'll always be an England,
And England shall be free,
If England means as much to you
As England means to me.

(Ross Parker and Harry Par-Davies, 1940)

Our excitement reached fever pitch when the char-à-bancs came at night and took us downtown to see the lights. We climbed onto those huge buses with much noise and chatter. Reverend Mother chuckled. "Come, my darlings," she said, patting the window seat beside her. I held on to Hazil and the two of us snuggled in there.

As the bus driver drove downtown and along the main street, to our left we looked out at the pier and the harbor beyond. Lights twinkled on boats, on the pier, and in the stores.

A few days later we were back at the pier again, this time to see a pantomime—a wonderful show that actors had managed to keep going all through the war—where the comedians taught us simple little songs with a great deal of clowning such as:

When can I have a banana again tell me mother do?
When can I have a banana again like I used to do?
I'd like one for breakfast, I'd like one for lunch

I'd like to eat a whole big bunch!
So when can I have a banana again,
Tell me mother do?

(Anonymous)

The first part of the show consisted of slapstick comedy and the second half of fairy tales, such as Cinderella or Little Red Riding Hood.

The victory celebrations went on and on. Grown-ups and children alike walked with a spring in their step. Then, too soon, we settled back into a routine of regular classes and regular chores. Reverend Mother went back to Thames Ditton, telling us that she intended to buy a new home there for us and as soon as it was ready, we'd all return.

13

Evacuees, the Sea and Manor Gardens

1945–1948:

In Torquay, homes for children abounded—Salvation Army homes, the St. Vincent de Paul Home for Boys and several others. The St. Vincent de Paul boys outnumbered the rest of us. The town and its surrounds were awash with children, as we didn't all return to our homes directly after the war. In fact, those of us from Thames Ditton stayed in Torquay for almost three and a half years.

Often when out for walks, we met the St. Vincent boys and the nuns who cared for them. "Good afternoon Sister," the sisters said to one another as we passed. The sisters of St. Vincent de Paul far outdid the sisters of St. Agnes in numbers and headdress. Large starched white wings sprouted from each side of their heads and bobbed and waved, like giant seagulls ready for takeoff, whereas our sisters wore veils that merely flapped gently in the breeze.

Sometimes we met at the cinema where the managers put on special matinees for the evacuees. Hundreds of us filed in to see films like *Billy the Kid*, which had me trembling with fright as cowboys hid behind buildings and shot at each other. We watched Walt Disney movies and tears splashed down our cheeks when

Bambi learned from his father that his mother had been taken away by "man."

Then there were outings to the beach and Manor Gardens. Often Sister asked us which we preferred—the beach or the gardens. My preference was always Manor Gardens—a beautiful, secluded woodland alive with wild flowers.

One Saturday when it had been decided to go to the beach we set out with buckets and spades, baskets of sandwiches, and other goodies for Meadfoot beach—for some, a treat—but for us who feared the water, a nightmare! Sister settled herself in her deckchair.

"Mary and Shirley, spread the blanket out please," and the boys carrying the baskets placed them on the blanket close to Sister.

"Brian you take Johnny, and Shirley you take Mary," Sister ordered. She insisted that we completely immerse ourselves in the sea as soon as we arrived; if not we'd get a cold, she said.

"I'll get wet on my own Sister, I will—I promise," I stated with some bravado.

"Off you go then."

I made my way to the water's edge, shivering more from fear than cold. I willed myself to go it alone, determined not to be pulled in anymore. Troubled by Ada's abuse, although she had returned to Thames Ditton, thoughts of being swept out to sea and not being able to swim back haunted me. The sea that had thrilled me when I first saw it was now my archenemy. I heard some of the children screaming with fright as others pulled them in, but I had to concentrate on my own endeavors and down I went splashing the water over me between gasps and shivers. Once this requirement was fulfilled, those who did not like the sea could play in the sand. Happily I ran up the beach.

"I'm all wet, Sister." My knitted swim suit hung down to my knees as proof that I had obeyed. Hazil and one or two others stood with me—all of us shivering with our teeth chattering.

"You can get a bucket and spade now," she said. Content, we settled down to build a sandcastle, digging, shoveling, and shaping. We ran here and there to gather seaweed, driftwood, shells, and stones to make the windows, doors, and a moat. Around four o'clock Sister called, "Teatime children, rinse your hands." We ran to the water's edge wriggling our hands in the waves, then sat in close proximity on the blanket and ate sandwiches with a certain amount of sand which we doused down with orange juice. We pulled on shirts and blouses, slipped into our sandals, made sure we carried what we had brought with us, and trudged uphill all the way home.

"Well," Sister said as we entered the cottage, "let's get everything put away and then go to the garden for awhile." The garden meant Gardener Grimshaw's well-kept lawn with its thick, lush grass. Playtime on the lawn—chasing around with Scruff and each other—soon dried out our knitted swimsuits and most of the sand brushed off.

Gardener Grimshaw kept a good garden, but in the meantime he continued to molest me and, I later learned, some of the other girls. He grew a bountiful array of fruits and vegetables. There were strawberries, apples, pears, carrots, and cabbages, and in the greenhouse peaches and tomatoes.

Mr. Morgan, the warden, looked after the apiary in the apple orchard and many times we saw him with his protective beekeeper headgear collecting honeycombs. And thanks to him, we often enjoyed bread and honey at teatime.

Summer days were pleasant.

By 1946, BBC had a nightly broadcast of *Dick Barton, Special Agent*. We had a radio in the cottage and Sister allowed us to listen to the marvelous adventures of this fictional hero. I think the whole of England listened.

Another love was Manor Gardens, which held a special secret that I never shared with anyone. On one occasion we walked there, wending our way through Lyncourt's gardens and descending a flight of steps that brought us to the lower Lincombe Road. To access the gardens, we pushed through a wrought iron gate that squeaked on its hinges. How I loved this woodland fairyland. Giant trees stood on each side of the pathway forming an arch over us. The path, packed hard with damp earth, meandered its way down to the seafront. The smell of wild flowers and especially bluebells filled our nostrils. In certain spots the sunlight filtered high above us through the treetops.

Scruffy always came with us, wagging his tail and giving short barks in anticipation of things to come. When we reached the clearing, the boys placed the picnic baskets on the table near the shelter and we waited for Sister to give us permission to play a game we loved called "Pom-Pom." We never tired of it. Pom-Pom gave us freedom to chase through the woods, climb trees and slide down the embankments. The challenge was to find a hiding place and then make it back to the clearing without being touched or seen by the catcher.

"Who is going to start today? Sister asked.

"I will," Alan offered. And with that we were running in every direction as we heard Alan yelling the countdown.

I scrambled up the bank, pushing through tall bracken, crossed a path, and crouched in tall grasses behind a huge tree. Panting I waited, listening for the moment when I would make a bolt for the clearing and get there without Alan catching me.

"Coming," I heard the cry far below, but suddenly a bright light pierced its way through the trees and captured my attention. I shaded my eyes and looked up. The light sent shimmering rays from its center but I could not look for long at the brightness. I wrapped my arms around my knees; it seemed time stood still. I felt as if a strong hand rested on my back and beautiful warmth penetrated my whole being. Exuberant, I stood up and leapt down the incline toward the shelter as if I had wings. But how could I tell anyone? I couldn't.

14

Audley Park School for Girls

September 1945:

The bell rang and girls emerged from the classrooms to enter the school quadrangle. I stood with my class waiting for our teacher to give us the nod. I watched the senior girls filing in silence toward the auditorium. On this my first day in senior school, at the age of eleven, my status reversed and I found myself once again among the youngest. Miss Baker, our teacher, had instructed us in the school's protocol. No running in the corridor, no talking going from class to class or assembly, show respect for teachers, hold doors open for anyone more senior than ourselves, obey to prefects and the head girl, and so on and so forth.

"Also," she said, "for those interested in music, you'll have opportunity to audition for the school choir, but not until you're in second year. Our choir is well-known and has a good reputation in the town. The school is divided into four houses, Nightingale, Curie, Cavell and Fry. These are the names of women of integrity who gave much to society and you will be learning about them in your history lessons. You will be assigned to one of the houses, and in everything you do you are expected to work at gaining points for your house. At the end of each month the house that you are in will meet in the auditorium to receive an update of its performance."

All this information I mulled over in my mind as I stood in line. It excited me; my world was changing and new and marvelous things were afoot. Our class started to move forward with Miss Baker leading the way. Only the sound of many shoes could be heard. Proudly I donned the school uniform that Reverend Mother had bought me. I wore a white blouse, green and black tie, black gym tunic, knee-high black socks, and matching shoes that shone. Miss Baker pointed to the lines on the floor of the auditorium. "Make sure your toes touch this line," she said. "I want to see a neat row." Why did such ritual thrill me? It was the order, the feeling of security and the expectancy of positive things ahead.

The Headmistress ascended the podium and addressed the school, welcoming the new students. The head girl read a Scripture and the music mistress led us in a hymn. A brief blessing was bestowed upon us and then we were dismissed for classes.

I did well in all subjects except for math, which to me was a conundrum. I sat embarrassed beyond measure when Miss Worthy unexpectedly stood by my desk. She reached down and took the book that I had been reading out of my hand and read in a loud voice, "The Mystery Boy of Castaway Isle." The class laughed while I wished the floor would swallow me up.

Eventually I joined the choir. I entered the music room for my audition, a little apprehensive, but determined to make it. I loved music with a passion. I had heard the choir sing and been thrilled at the songs and harmonies of their voices. I wanted to be a member.

"Which hymn would you like to sing dear?" asked the kindly music mistress. I chose "Fight the good fight with all thy might. Christ is thy strength and Christ thy right." I sang with confidence and my reward was acceptance into the Audley Park school choir. With elation I ran home to tell Sister.

Our choir sang in music festivals and sometimes joined other school choirs to sing rousing pieces, including my favorite, "Liberty," sung to the music of "Elgar's 4th Pomp and Circumstance March." Mr.

Robinson, our passionate conductor, tapped his baton on the podium to bring us to attention. "Watch me children, watch me."

When we came to the magnificent final stanza, singing: "*God is drawing His sword,*" he swept his baton across his chest as if drawing his own sword from its sheath. And with great gusto, we continued: "*We are marching with the Lord. Sing then brothers, sing.*" The air electric, he brought us to a rousing end.

I had a friend in school who stood beside me in those invigorating music festivals. She loved music too. A few days after the festival, I heard her calling to me as I walked along the school corridor. I waited. She couldn't move fast because of the heavy iron braces she had to wear on her legs, causing her body to swing from side to side.

"Mary, Mary did you see the notice board in our classroom? You won an award in the Torquay art contest."

"I did?" Together we rushed to see the postings. My teacher Miss Baker sat at her desk in the classroom and smiled.

"Come on in girls. You can have a look." And there I read, "Mary Melloy, Highly Commended."

All the winning entries were eventually displayed in the town hall. Reverend Mother, who sometimes came to Torquay for short visits, took me to see the exhibition.

"You're doing well, my darling," she said as we stood together looking at my painting of three Spitfires. I'd carefully painted the red, white and blue circles on each of the wing tips. She put her arm around me and gave me a hug.

My school encouraged participation in sports, for me another exhilarating activity. I excelled in track and field. The day came when I marched with my teammates around the town stadium at the start of our summer games.

I felt so small as I looked up at the bleachers. People appeared as dots. I strained my eyes searching for the familiar black and white of Reverend Mother and Sister St. Claire's garb. Later in the day when all the races were done, I was still jubilant at the thought of how I had pulled far ahead of my competitors in the third leg of the relay race, securing a victory for our school. "Did you see me Reverend Mother? Did you see?"

"I saw you," she said, cupping my face in her hands and kissing the tip of my nose.

15

Back to Thames Ditton

1948–1950:

"Children, you're coming home." We the children sat in the sitting room in Lyncourt and listened to Reverend Mother. "It's been a long time, but at last your new home is ready," she said. "What do you think of that?" She looked from one to the other, her face alight with that familiar smile.

"Where exactly is our new home?" I asked.

"It's so close you'll be able to walk to the Home of Compassion and come for tea," she said.

We had been in Devon for several years. I had been six when we arrived and now my fourteenth birthday loomed a few months away. Why did I feel misgivings about this news? There were so many things I had come to love about Torquay and now it would be an adjustment to move back to Thames Ditton.

I lay in bed that night and thought about the places that I had come to hold so dear—not only in Torquay, but all of Devon. I loved the winding roads, the landscape, the palm trees, Manor Gardens with its host of bluebells in the spring, and the yellow primroses and other flowers of that magical place. Even the ferocious sea held a charm for me; though gray and sullen in the wintertime, it sparkled with a variety of blues and turquoises in the spring and summer sun.

Would there be a garden in Thames Ditton like Miss Marden's of Torquay? She was a kind, elderly lady, with silver-gray hair and a soft voice, who lived a few houses down from Lyncourt. On warm summer evenings, we were invited to walk in her walled garden. I loved the crunch of the gravel pathway under my feet as we walked sedately along, where roses climbed up the trellises and where wall-flowers with their velvety petals and deep rich shades of red and yellow sent forth wonderful perfumes. Would I write any more poems in our new home as I had to the sea, the flowers, and woodlands?

Hot tears threatened. I lay on my back, willing myself to continue my reverie. Mrs. Marden's house put me in mind of the land-army girls who lived next door to her. They had given us a festive victory party after the war ended.

And what about Miss Cotton—a genteel lady who came to the cottage and told us the amazing adventures of a little pink elephant? She made the adventures up as she went along and we always told her where she'd left off the next time she came. Miss Cotton also treated some of us to tea at the Drum Inn in the medieval village of Cockington, where she indulged us in strawberries and real Devon clotted cream. And afterwards we walked to the forge and watched the blacksmith hammering away at horseshoes.

I let my mind wander further and smiled in the dark as I thought about the memorable day trips—trips when we clambered onto char-à-bancs with our packed lunches and drove to Cornwall to play on the wide sandy beaches of Bude and walk the quaint villages of Looe and Polperro; trips to Dartmoor and Buckfast Abbey with its ancient monastery; trips that gave us a bird's-eye view of the Devonshire landscape.

Then there were times when we rose early on misty autumn mornings before school or breakfast and trekked the back roads of the Lincombes until we came to a wooded slope where we'd gather walnuts, with Scruffy bounding between us, giving affectionate licks as we pocketed our spoil! I'd miss it all.

Tomorrow's Saturday, I thought as I lay there. *Peggy will be coming!* I knew I would sorely miss Peggy, our maid who came in five and a half days a week to clean the cottage. I treasured the times when Sister sent me to help Peggy change the beds and dust and sweep on Saturday mornings, because Peggy loved me and I loved Peggy. I had fun helping her, especially when she tickled me in between chores.

I'd say in a sing-song voice, "I'm not going to help you."

"If you don't—I'll tickle you," Peggy would sing back with a twinkle in her eye. And tickle she did, until I rolled on one of the beds, helpless with laughter. *Tomorrow will be good day*, I thought.

But the day came when Peggy, Elsie, Sister Faith, and others gathered to help Sister St. Claire in closing up the cottage as they sorted bedding, clothing, and tableware. They lined up the big trunks and packed each accordingly.

Moving day came soon enough and we rode in taxis to Torquay station. Never having seen a steam train before, the noise of it terrified some of the smaller children and caused loud cries and tears, but there were plenty of helpers to reassure. Sister St. Claire had designated two adults and six children to a compartment. We boarded the train—the step so high the little ones had to be lifted up. Hazil was almost eleven and mounted the train easily. Together we followed our designate Sister Faith along the corridor into our compartment. I was glad to have Hazil with me. "Do you want to sit by the window?" I asked her. She nodded and pressed her face to the glass.

The picnic baskets packed with our lunches were placed on the racks above our heads by Gardener Grimshaw—he grinning and making remarks about how much he'd miss us as he exited.

The train started to slowly pull out of the station. Sister allowed us to go back into the corridor and wave to those on the platform. Most returning our waves would eventually join us in Thames Ditton, but not dear Peggy, as her roots were in Devon. My eyes smarted as I thought about the finality of our good-byes.

I went back to my seat, put an arm around Hazil and stared out at the red soil of Devon and at the sea as the train rattled through Dawlish and other coastal towns. "Good-bye Torquay, good-bye," I whispered.

Some hours later we arrived at Thames Ditton Station where Mr. Cattermole waited with his fleet of cars. "Welcome back—my how you've grown," he said with a warm smile. Soon we pulled up in front of black wrought iron gates that were wide open. Reverend Mother stood at the door of a big white house with her arms outstretched. We tumbled out of the cars and ran up the pathway. She bent down hugging and kissing the little ones.

"How's my Mary?" she said, looking up at me with her beautiful brown eyes.

"Very well, thank you Reverend Mother," I said as I curtsied. To grant her the respect she commanded, all the nuns, maids, and we girls as we matured were expected to curtsy to her and likewise the men and boys saluted or raised their caps and she always inclined her head in acknowledgment.

"Come in my darlings. Come and see your new home." We entered a spacious house with a large foyer. To our right the dining room displayed oil paintings in pastel shades—all depicted cherubs with garlands of flowers. The paintings reached from ceiling to the cream molding, with each set in an alcove. The far end of the room jutted out like a half tower with windows that extended from ceiling to floor. Beyond I could see the walled garden. Next to the dining room the refectory boasted a swag plaster ceiling with clusters of fruits intertwined with cherubs and roses.

We had a tour of the whole house and were amazed at the many rooms on the upper levels. One had been converted into a chapel, and adjacent to it, a library was stacked with secondhand books. I often visited the library and many times Sister reprimanded me for taking books up to my bedroom, hiding some under my mattress and reading others under the covers with the aid of a flashlight.

Of the house called *Newlands*, I learned in later years that the site on which it stood had at one time been sold by the Abbess of Barking to Henry VIII, and that lords and ladies from a later era had also owned the property. To acquire this property for us, Reverend Mother had exchanged Boyle Farm Cottage where we had lived before the war. *Newlands* now became *St. Agnes Home for Children*.

Reverend Mother had additions built onto the house consisting of a large playroom, washrooms, a cloakroom, and a small concert hall. The concert hall served as a source of much needed income. Groups in the village and further afield rented it for weddings, meetings, and music practices. On a summer evening, Sister would allow us to sit on the fire escape stairs and listen to the D'Oyly Carte Opera Company practicing Gilbert and Sullivan operas. Their voices rang out, floating on the evening air. These sessions delighted us. Hazil and I and others sang together, "I'm called little Buttercup, dear little Buttercup," and other songs from the operas as we gathered in the nursery or even while we did chores. The Company always gave tickets for us to attend the matinee and by the time we saw the show, we knew many of the songs by heart.

My interest in art, theater, and music increased. Reverend Mother arranged for me to have piano lessons and came to hear me play in the recitals. My art teacher thought I should enroll in art school. However, Reverend Mother did not agree. My piano lessons came to naught as I did not use practice time wisely. Instead I wrote songs and poetry about the flowers, birds, and bees—none of which helped me to become proficient on the piano.

I had become a dreamer. I heard my first pop song at sixteen years of age and Bing Crosby's melodic voice resonated in my head. He sang about "faraway places with strange sounding names." I started to wonder about the bigger world out there.

On Sundays we walked through the peaceful village of Thames Ditton, making our way to the Home of Compassion. Up the gravel driveway we went and in quiet reverence we traversed the cloisters and entered the chapel. Inside statues of Jesus, the Virgin Mary, and the apostles stood in the silence. And high up, the sun pierced through the stained-glass windows. Many of the patients were wheeled in their beds to the chapel. Staff and people from the village attended the services too. Some of we children sang in the choir and at Christmas time the chapel would be packed as friends, relatives, and residents came to see us perform a nativity play. In these performances, I was in my element.

In contrast, school became a place of misery for me. I now attended a large co-ed school. I had never seen so many males, great strapping fellows who were loud and boisterous. How I longed for my quiet, orderly girls' school and the good manners that were expected of each pupil. I became withdrawn, shy, and overwhelmed with the milieu that confronted me.

One spark of light, however, shone in my life at that time—Mrs. Brewster. How I looked forward to this Australian teacher's art class. Her two daughters attended the school too. Mrs. Brewster befriended me and admired my artwork, sometimes praising me in front of the class. "There's a girl in this front row," she said one time, "who works very hard and gets good results for her efforts." My spirits lifted as I realized her kindness. "Mary—I want to speak to you after class," she announced on one occasion. I waited until the last student left the classroom before speaking to her, a little nervous at being centered out. Mrs. Brewster had the bluest eyes—periwinkle blue. Her eyes reminded me of the warmth of Elsie, our cook in Torquay.

"I'd like to invite you to our home, "she said. "Why don't you come early on Saturday morning and stay the whole day? Mr. Connor, the art master for the boys and I have both said we'd like to paint your portrait. Would you mind sitting for us for awhile and then you and the girls can have some time together."

Would I mind! I hoped Sister St. Claire would allow me to go. "Thank you Mrs. Brewster. I'll have to ask Sister if she'll let me come," I said shyly.

"Why don't I call and ask her?" she said. And she did.

The more I visited, the more I became at ease with Mrs. Brewster, her husband, their two daughters, and Mr. Connor. I was fascinated with the close and fun relationship the girls had with their dad. I witnessed the interactions of a happy and well adjusted family. After several visits, feeling more at ease, I even shared with Mrs. Brewster my passion for the arts. She always listened attentively. "You never know, Mary," she'd say.

As for the portraits, Mr. Connor announced one day, "Mary, I'm not going to insult you anymore. I just can't capture you on paper." But Mrs. Brewster completed hers and gave it to me as a gift. My times with this kindhearted lady and her family provided a pleasant escape for me from the school.

16

Restless Souls

Sister St. Claire continued to be in charge of the children's home. The remaining staff stayed in Torquay for some time and returned later with the rest of the elderly patients to settle once again in the Home of Compassion.

Reverend Mother assigned two nursery nurses and two live-in maids to the children's home. There were approximately 20 children, and Ann and I, now in our teens, were the oldest. We were assigned household duties such as helping the smaller children with washing and dressing, and on Saturday mornings changing beds and dusting.

There were times when Sister's Irish temper exploded. On reflection, with some of us chomping at the bit, this should not have been surprising. The day Miss Senior, one of our benefactors, brought two bikes to the home triggered an event that caused Sister St. Claire to vent her fury. Often our days were interrupted with visitors or well-wishers coming to the home with donations of items such as cots, toys and clothing. It was Saturday morning and Ann and I were upstairs cleaning bedrooms and bathrooms. On hearing the doorbell we crept to the top of the stairs and peeped through the banisters.

"The bikes will be a useful addition," we heard Sister say. "The older children will be able to cycle to the village when I need extra supplies."

"You're most welcome," we heard Miss Senior respond, "but I must be on my way." And with that she walked toward the front door. As Miss Senior left we crept back up the stairs, avoiding the ones that creaked.

"Mary and Ann!" the sound of Sister's voice floated up the stairwell.

"Yes Sister?" We clattered down the stairs trying to feign the right amount of surprise. She eyed us with suspicion and we knew she was aware of our eavesdropping.

"I want you to take these bikes to the shed," she said, handing me a large bunch of keys.

"They're lovely bikes, aren't they Sister?" Ann said.

"They are ordinary and practical and no one will ride them without my permission. Have you girls finished cleaning?"

"We still have two rooms and the end bathroom," I volunteered.

"Perhaps if you hadn't been wasting time at the top of the stairs you'd be further ahead."

I made no reply, but struggled to keep the matronly bike with its wicker basket upright as I followed Ann down the passageway and out of the back door.

Upstairs far away from Sister, we resumed our tasks. Ann sang as she rubbed the duster up and down on the chest of drawers:

"When you ride a bicycle, watch out for the motorcars.
When you ride a bicycle never take your hands off the handle bars."

She looked across the six-bedded room to where I was energetically stuffing dirty linen into a large laundry bag. Then she went on singing:

"Pedal slowly to and fro, you'll get where you want to go.

Don't do tricks you think you know, because you saw them at the show."

As I pulled the bag across the floor I joined loudly in the last stanza:

"Keep cool as an icicle, when you ride a bicycle."

We had learned the song at one of the pantomimes.

"I know a way," Ann said.

After our chores were finished we hurried downstairs to help prepare the smaller children for lunch. Mealtimes were orderly affairs. In single file we went from playroom to dining room and stood behind our chairs until Sister sat down.

The day progressed and by 7:00 p.m. the smaller children had settled for the night. The eleven to thirteen-year-olds joined Sister in the refectory and watched television shows. By eight they too were dismissed and sent to bed. Ann and I had one last job—to take our Scruffy for a walk. My spirits lifted as I thought about the pleasure of it. I loved Scruffy—he had been through the war with us and was fiercely loyal. He would bark furiously and try to pull Sister's arm away whenever she spanked us and he remained an affectionate and faithful companion to all.

By nine the two resident maids sat in their armchairs dozing in the kitchen. I walked along the passageway; Scruffy lay in the hallway, one ear cocked. "Scruffy come 'walkies' then," I whispered. I bent down and ran my fingers through his thick coat. He thumped his tail on the floor then stood and stretched; his bright, intelligent eyes watched me closely.

"And bike riding," Ann said softly as she came up behind me. My heart flipped.

I knocked on the refectory door, poked my head in and told Sister we were going to take Scruff for his walk.

Outside, the night breeze rustled through the tall trees surrounding the property; we moved quickly past the scullery and then the pantry windows. Ann stopped at the shed; with a small penknife she removed the screws that held the lock plate to the door. Within seconds the lock, still intact, swung from the doorframe. Scruff yelped with impatience. "Shush, Scruff," I implored. I pulled him back on his leash and Ann wheeled the bike with the wicker basket out of the shed. To avoid walking in front of the house we crossed the road, making a wide circle, and backtracked, accessing the quiet street that ran parallel to the south side of the house.

"Here goes!" Ann announced, and she mounted the bike with relative ease. I trotted alongside her as she made her precarious start. Scruffy barked excitedly at my heels.

Soon she rode at a fair speed and left me behind. Cycling back toward me, she said, "Your turn. You have to keep pedaling and make sure the handlebars are straight. It's a great feeling."

With some trepidation, I tried to mount. Ann struggled to keep the bike upright and the more she did, the more I failed, and the more we laughed. Eventually I pedaled away unsteadily. Picking up speed I became more confident. I turned to cycle back to Ann, concentrating on keeping the bars in alignment. As I did I stared in disbelief. In one blinding flash I saw Sister. As if in an instant of time, her familiar rolling gait, like a nightmare, came toward me, her white veil flapping in the night wind. The road came up to meet me as I crashed at her feet.

Scruffy licked my face whining softly as I struggled up. I took his leash from Ann while she lifted the bike. No words were spoken until Sister said, "Get back to the house girls." We walked in silence and finally stood before her in the refectory. She had us relate to her how we'd procured the bicycle.

"I'm ashamed of you. You're supposed to be an example to the smaller children and now it appears I can't trust you." She went on to say our punishment would be going to bed at the same time

as the little ones for one week. This seemed bearable as I thought
of how I could read the books I had stored away. But her last decision, like a knife in my heart, forced me to blink back tears that
threatened to fall. I coughed and sniffed. We were to be denied
the pleasure of taking Scruff for his nightly walk; two of the boys
would do it. Ann remained unrepentant, staring defiantly ahead.
Sister's eyes burned with anger and with a swift move she rose to
her feet, striking Ann across her face. "Get out," she ordered. The
order did not need repeating and we flew to the sanctity of our
bedroom, while Scruff sat on his haunches in the hallway and bale-
fully howled.

Ann lay on her bed, her hands tucked behind her head, and
stared at the ceiling. "We did ride a bike though," she said quietly.
I smiled a little and sighed as she sang softly with a little crack in
her voice: "*Keep cool as an icicle when you ride a bicycle.*"

17

Transition

I had completed senior school and now sat in Reverend Mother's sitting room listening to her wise counsel, although I didn't think it wise counsel at the time.

"I want to sing and be an actress," I told her. I perceived concern in her expression, but the love of music and art remained with me.

Reverend Mother said there were issues she wanted to discuss with me. "Mary you know you're very special to me," she said, with a catch in her voice. "I adopted you when you were two and I promised I would direct you and help you to the best of my ability. I don't need to tell you a lot about your mother, but she did ask to see you when you were fifteen—but I decided against it." This news shocked me. So my mother had cared—at least some.

"Why Reverend Mother, why couldn't I see her?"

She didn't answer me directly, but instead said, "Mary—I want you to take great care when you go out. There are many evil people in the world and young girls are snatched away. Don't ever walk along the edge of the pavement when you're in town, a car could pull alongside and the driver kidnap you." I felt this had something to do with my mother. Did she want me that much?

Reverend Mother went on to tell me that my mother's husband had been a kind man and in fact had come to the home to see me as a baby. However, the issue at hand concerned my future. Reverend Mother had decided I should be a nurse and she had already sent for and received information from the West London School of Nursing about its training program.

"I couldn't be a nurse," I wailed, "I want to go to art school." But in this Reverend Mother remained resolute; she told me her plan. I would work in her Home of Compassion for one year to learn the basics of nursing care and then an application would be made to the school. "Oh, no," I cried.

"My Mary, do you realize I won't always be here for you? One day I'll be gone and I want to make sure you have a good profession and will be able to take care of yourself." I said nothing, and just stood there, sulking. She spoke again. "I had hoped that you might come and work in the home when you've done your training."

Anger rose in my heart.

Reverend Mother looked at me with worried eyes. "Suppose you agree to do your nurse's training and if you really don't like it then you can go to art school." Suddenly the enormity of what she had done for me and the other children struck home. I realized how much she cared and how much she loved me. My rebellion dissipated, I got up and hugged her, and we rocked and cried together as I said, "I'll try Reverend Mother. I'll try."

18

New Beginnings

The year 1952 brought a time of new beginnings for Ann and me. We were no longer considered children and our emerging womanhood could not be denied. Reverend Mother included us among her guests at St. Veronica's, a charming thatched cottage in the village of Bembridge on the Isle-of-Wight.

The cottage had eight tiny bedrooms. Each room had a name—the pink room, the blue room, the floral room and so on, obviously depicting their decor. The main floor had two sitting rooms and the refectory; and at the back the kitchen and pantry. The hard wooden floors were polished to a sheen by the maids who arrived at the cottage at the beginning of each season to clean.

Reverend Mother had a loyal group of supporters and they had enabled her to buy the cottage. She and the nuns enjoyed a retreat there in the summer months. Supporters of the home and their families rented the cottage at times. They enjoyed a vacation and the money served to help with the expenses for the upkeep of the Home of Compassion and St. Agnes Home for Children.

St. Veronica's in long ago days had belonged to smugglers. With the sea a few hundred yards away, it had been an ideal spot for such activity. But now it belonged to Reverend Mother and her Sisters of Mercy. The sisters had all returned to Thames Ditton after a two-week retreat, except for Sister Monica. As was customary, Reverend Mother remained for one more week with invited guests, and for Ann and me this marked our first official holiday as grown ups.

On our first evening at suppertime, Ann and I assisted Dorothy, Reverend Mother's maid, with carrying dishes from the kitchen and placing them on the heavy oak table in the refectory. All that done, we sat in our places. Dorothy had been Reverend Mother's personal maid ever since I could remember; now worn down with arthritis, her frail body moved at a snail's pace and her heavy orthopedic shoes slowed her pace even more. She stood in the doorway, a large grin on her face as her wide blue eyes scanned the seven of us seated at the table.

"At's evryfing Reverend Muvver." She had no teeth to pronounce the "th." Wisps of limp gray hair had escaped her once stiffly starched cap, which now sagged with the onslaught of steam and heat it had endured in the kitchen; hands red and roughened by domestic work hung loosely by her side.

"Thank you, Dorothy." Reverend Mother inclined her head in dismissal. And Dorothy went with the two Airedale dogs trotting after her for their evening feed.

Father Scammell, one of Reverend Mother's guests, asked the blessing and we helped ourselves to food.

"Are you enjoying nursing school Mary?" he asked.

"Yes, thank you Father. I really do like it now and I did well in the exams."

Reverend Mother, seated at the top of the table, smiled her approval. The exams had been the preliminary ones that had determined whether I could go into formal training. I decided not to tell Reverend Mother that my sister tutor at the hospital the week before exams had read out the names of more than half the class—mine included—predicting we would fail, and fortunately for me her forecast did not come true.

Mrs. Scammell, the mother of Father Scammell, spoke, "You are going to do very well, dear." The warmth of her voice matched the warmth of her personality. She beamed and nodded at me across the table; laugh lines fanned out from her eyes and disappeared into rosy plump cheeks while the gray bun on the top of her head threatened to topple. "Don't you think Mary will make a good nurse?" she said to her son.

"I'm quite sure of it." The Anglican priest's smile melted my heart. Ann and I had a crush on the good father and discussed his every attribute in our private teenage world. I knew that later on we would lie on our beds with our youthful legs stretched up on the delicate flowered wallpaper and talk about him. Although this hailed our emergence into the world of grown-ups, the whims of youth had not completely departed. He spoke then to Ann. "Perhaps you'll be a nurse too."

"I'm thinking about it," she said.

"Would you really like nursing school dear?" Reverend Mother asked. "It would make me so happy to know you'll both have secure futures."

More conversation ensued about Ann going to nursing school and by the time we finished the meal she decided she would apply.

There were some agonizing moments to those meals on our first grown-up holiday. One of Reverend Mother's guests, Miss Clancy, wore ill-fitting false teeth. Ann had named her "Miss Clutter-Teeth" and to avoid breaking into uncontrollable laughter when she started to noisily cluck away, we tried to keep conversations going during the meal. With some conniving on our part, Reverend Mother and Sister Monica would relate the tale of how the nuns had first purchased the property and of how they had found bottles of rum in the well in the back garden. We were not always successful in our efforts and sometimes resorted to loud sneezes and coughing to cover up our naughtiness.

And then one evening over dinner we discussed a drama at sea that had occurred the previous night.

Ann spoke, "It must be so scary for the people at sea when a storm hits."

"I didn't hear a thing until Ann banged on my door," I said. Lost in thought for a moment, I wondered what it was like for people who drowned at sea. Ada's cruelty in holding my head beneath the water as a child flashed into my mind and coldness enveloped me. Father Scammell's voice brought me back to the present.

"It was about two in the morning when the siren went off," he said. "A distress signal sounded from a boat out at sea."

One of the villagers, on his way to the sea, had rattled our gate, shouting, "Ship in distress!" Following tradition upon hearing the siren, the villagers, including all of us, had dressed quickly and hurried down to the beach to watch and pray. We arrived to see the lifeboat crew running along the pier that stretched out into the sea. Everyone strained to see the boat as it slid down the ramp into the choppy waters and disappeared from view.

We stood there, clutching blankets and shawls close to ourselves for protection against the howling winds and lashing rain. Some prayed out loud. Others just stared into the darkness. We returned to our homes for a while, only to come back to the beach again to wait and pray. When the weary crew returned and announced all were rescued, a loud cheer went up.

"Thank God for a successful mission," Father Scammell said.

Reverend Mother spoke quietly. "Indeed, "she said, "yes indeed."

Dinner over, Ann and I piled plates and dishes onto the little trolley that stood in the corner of the refectory, wheeled it to the kitchen, and set to washing and putting away the dishes while Dorothy took care of the leftover food, placing it in containers.

With anticipation, Reverend Mother's Airedale dogs paced the small passageway, punctuating the air with short, sharp barks, knowing that soon we would take them for a walk. I heard Reverend Mother laugh as she came into the kitchen swinging the dogs' leashes back and forth. "What's this?" she said, bending down and patting them.

"We're ready, Reverend Mother," I said, taking the leashes and handing one to Ann. We clipped them onto the dogs' collars and made our way out of St. Veronica's, crossed the road, and proceeded along the laneway that ran parallel with the sea. The sun, warm on our backs, with all evidence of the storm gone, made for a pleasant evening stroll. Miss Clancy, Sister Monica and Father Scammell accompanied us, while Dorothy and Mrs. Scammell stayed in the cottage.

The ensuing years brought us to the island many times. We snapped pictures of ourselves at Blackgang Chine, once the haunt of smugglers and now a huge amusement park, and Carisbrooke Castle, among other attractions.

The holiday over, I returned to London and focused on the serious business of becoming a registered nurse. My world expanded; many students came from overseas, especially medical students. On our arrival a welcome party took place in the residence for the medical and nursing students. The sister tutors and the resident surgeon made polite conversation with us. Alarmed at so many men, I retreated to a corner. A pleasant Nigerian came and introduced himself to me. "Hello, I'm James." He stretched out his hand and I struggled to suppress my shyness as I responded, saying, "I'm Mary." James and I dated on and off, but eventually I broke off the relationship, because I couldn't love him the way he declared he loved me. But for many weeks I received a letter from him with every mail delivery, which came three times a day!

As time went on the whole group came to know each other well. We worked together on the wards, dined in the cafeteria, and went out socially to dances and the theater. And being students, we got into mischief on occasions. The nursing students were allowed one late pass a week up to 11:00 p.m. If we were later than that, we couldn't get into the residence because a wrought iron railing with a locked gate surrounded the building and thick bushes ran the length of the railings. The medical students, however, had bent two of the railings to the extent a slim little nursing student could wriggle through and gain entrance through the back door!

The practical aspects of nursing were learned on the wards. Each year we spent three months in the classroom and nine months on the wards. Partnered with a senior nurse in our first year, we were introduced to every aspect of nursing care. By our second year we were more confident and began mentoring first-year students.

At the end of my second year I was assigned the night shift on a small convalescent ward, the problem being that the four or five patients recuperating there were completely self-sufficient and needed little nursing intervention. "It's so boring," I complained to my roommate. I cut gauze swabs and packed the steel drums ready for sterilization, cleaned the small utility room, and read study books in an effort to stay awake and alert. But as soon as I started to read, my eyes crossed and my chin sunk into my chest. I would come to with a start and jump up to pace the floor.

"I've heard that nurses assigned to that ward sleep in the armchair," my friend said. "The night sisters don't do a 2:00 a.m. round there." The next night I tried it. I thought, *I'll lay back and try to read*; however, in the wee hours of the morning, I felt someone standing over me but I could not move—it was night nurse's paralysis! The next thing I knew, I could hear the phone ringing. It rang many times before I could shake myself awake. I fumbled with the phone and at length put it to my ear.

"Stephen Paget Ward," I said, trying to sound alert.

"Nurse," the head night sister's voice came curtly through the phone line, "Sister Browning has just been to your unit and noted that you were asleep. You are to report to my office as soon as the day staff arrives."

My punishment comprised of a severe lecture, which lasted for a good fifteen minutes. Relieved beyond measure, I vowed to stay awake no matter what and prayed I'd soon be moved to a busy ward, where time just flew by. It happened soon enough—I was transferred to the ward simply known as "Casualty," the emergency area that was a beehive of activity. Being in London, the nighttime shift brought in drunks, car accident injuries, lacerations, knife wounds, and plenty of drama. If ever my nerves were tested it was there. We had all heard of how one of the student nuns, of which there were several, had been vigorously pursued around the department by a drunken Irishman one night when her co-worker had gone for a coffee break. I was relieved to learn that a male nurse or orderly now had to be in the department during night shifts.

One morning around 2:00 a.m. when emergency patients had been attended to and relative calm prevailed, I made my way to the cafeteria, poured a cup of tea, grabbed a biscuit, and looked around the almost empty room.

"Come and sit here nurse." A pretty blond staff-nurse had given me the invite. Usually student nurses chummed with those in their own year. It seemed an unwritten rule and somehow those at a senior level were distant. I had often noticed this staff-nurse—a quiet person with a gentleness about her and a warm smile. I sat down. "How are you? Do like Casualty?" she asked.

"I'm getting used to it, although it is hair-raising at times." I gave her a half smile, because I couldn't think of anything else to say. She made a few more comments then said she had to get back to the Dan Mason Wing. I knew that was a private ward for patients with money, who could afford extra niceties, such as little lace doilies on their trays and nurses to meet their every whim.

There came the day when I was assigned to the same ward as the staff-nurse, on the day shift. I came to know Ruth well, and she proved to be a good teacher as well as a caring person. She tolerated me and another nurse on the ward who talked frequently about David Whitfield, a truck driver turned pop star who sang romantic songs like *Cara Mia*. My interest in music continued and I now listened to a broader range of styles. And often I went to the cinema to see musicals, where I swooned over Mario Lanza singing in *The Great Caruso!*

Ruth reminded me of one of the student nuns—a friendly person who many times said to me and to others with her soft Irish lilt, "I'll pray for you my dear; that I will." Once Ruth asked me if I'd like to go to church with her but I declined, not feeling I had time for that. My friends and I were rehearsing every spare minute for the hospital's Christmas concert. Still struggling with shyness, I had gone to the first concert meeting to tell the producer I would like to help behind the scenes. I sat there listening to her explain that we would do a variety show, then a pantomime. She then started to point at various people, telling them what part she wanted them to practice. She looked at me and said, "You will do a calypso number with one of the fellows."

"I'm here to help behind the scenes," I said.

"Oh, no you're not, you're just right for the part I have in mind," she insisted. And that lady, being a professional actress, proceeded to coax me out of my shyness and taught me to dance well, along with Solomon, one of the doctors who at one point had to pick me up and swing me around. I enjoyed the excitement of those days and all the camaraderie that went with being a student in a close-knit community.

Later in the year, Ruth approached me again. "Billy Graham is coming to London for a crusade at Harringay Arena," she said. "Would you like to come?" I didn't want to, but I agreed I would go.

"I'm sure you'll enjoy it, Mary," Ruth said. When we arrived, I couldn't believe the vast numbers of people making their way into the arena. They came in droves. *Why so many?* I wondered. I followed Ruth up several flights of stairs before we found seats. My eyes scanned the crowd and then my attention was drawn to the choir as they began to sing. *What a heavenly sound. What magnificent music.* As the choir sung their last hymn and Billy Graham delivered his message of salvation, my mind wandered and I started to wish I'd gone to the dance with my friends. When he asked for people who didn't know Jesus as their personal Savior to go forward to make a commitment, I rebelled inwardly. Aware of Ruth quietly praying beside me, instead of feeling gratitude, I felt anger. I wanted to leave. Much water would pass under the bridge before that message would hit home.

Time pressed on and my 21st birthday dawned. Sister St. Claire organized a special birthday party for me. I invited almost twenty of my peers from the hospital—ten medical students and nine of my nursing friends. Tables were set up in the concert hall—the same one where the D'Oyly Carte Company practiced each year. Mrs. Styles, the cook, glowed as she served us roast chicken with all the trimmings. Sister St. Claire made the cake and she and Reverend Mother came to wish me happy birthday before leaving us young people to dance.

Another six months and my three-and-a-half years of training came to an end; I sat my final exams—passed—and returned to Thames Ditton. Reverend Mother waited for me and as I entered, she wrapped her arms around me. "Well done, my Mary," she said several times. "I'm so proud of you. Come on in darling. Dorothy, you can make the tea now."

I sat down in her familiar room. The table had already been set for two with Reverend Mother's fine china; a plate of thinly sliced bread and butter and a plate of cakes were placed in the center. Dorothy soon brought in the tea. As we ate, Reverend Mother told me the government had ordained that all privately-run children's homes had to have a trained nurse working in the facility. "Would you work in the children's home Mary?" What emotion I felt. Having tasted freedom of a sort, how could I settle down to being at the home again? I struggled inwardly. Reverend Mother

said, "How about a year? See how you feel at the end of that time."
And I agreed. I told her that I wanted to take two weeks' holiday
with Ann first, as we had planned to go to Torquay and stay at the
Torbay Hotel along the seafront.

We left the next weekend and visited all our old haunts—Lyncourt and the cottage, Meadfoot beach and Manor Gardens—all so
dear to my heart. And then I returned, with some misgiving, to St.
Agnes Home for Children as a staff member.

19

The Bird Must Fly

I returned to Newlands—St. Agnes Home for Children—to begin my duties in 1955. Sister St. Claire welcomed me. Although so different from hospital life, I learned to adjust. My charges were healthy children ranging in age from three to thirteen. A live-in nursery nurse took care of four babies.

Much was reminiscent of my teen years, except for the loss of dear Scruffy who had died just before I left for nursing school.

A new sense of responsibility reigned. I did a quick survey of the house and saw that many areas could be improved upon. The linen cupboard, a shambles of sheets and towels and other linens, needed a major overhaul. With the cupboard straightened out, I noticed a decrease in the number of sheets coming from the laundry each week. I discussed this with Sister and we noted the cook who came in daily, a Mrs. Granger, always volunteered to check and put the linen away. Unfortunately, it was revealed she put much of it away in her own home! The police dealt with the matter and we hired a new cook.

With the help of one of the nursery nurses, I tackled other areas. Clothes had been stuffed tightly into chests of drawers on the landings and in the bedrooms; much had been donated but little had seen its intended use. We sorted the clothes into sizes and allocated a drawer for each child. I arranged to have hooks put in the bathrooms where each child hung their own washcloth and towel. Tooth brushes and tooth mugs were placed in a row above the sinks.

I fulfilled my artistic bent by writing plays and songs for the children and we performed them as birthday gifts for Reverend Mother and Sister.

On my day off I took the train to London, a half-hour ride away, and started singing and ballet lessons. My ballet teacher arranged for me to have a small part in a film—a crowd scene. The camera was to zero in on me dancing to rock and roll music then pan out to embrace the whole scene—a house party!

It meant extra days off work, as I was required, along with other extras, to be on the set for three days. My stomach was in knots as I asked Sister St. Claire for the time off to travel to London for the filming; she had made it clear on many occasions that she thoroughly disapproved of my leisure time activities. I had already had extra time off to compete in a singing contest; not that I was "discovered," but the urge to try remained almost an obsession. With a clipped retort, Sister St. Claire told me to go and speak to Reverend Mother about my request, but not without first saying, "Your behavior is not becoming of a young lady." She added, "What sort of example are you to the children?" Resentment and anger burned within me.

"I just want to try. I like everything about show business," I responded.

"Don't be so ridiculous. You trained to be a nurse and you agreed to work here and that's what you should be focused on."

"Well I may not be here much longer," I shouted, "so you won't have to worry about what I do."

Sister's face blanched. I took one of the bikes and rode furiously to the village, my thoughts in a whirl. The idea of leaving grew strong in my mind. I could go and stay with Ann, my classmate and friend; she was married and lived nearby. I missed the social freedom I had enjoyed at the hospital. I'd get a job, maybe in another nursery. The work was easy and I wouldn't have to be answerable to anyone for my off-duty activities.

I arrived at the Home of Compassion with my mind already made up. "Well, my Mary," Reverend Mother said, "Sister St. Claire phoned me. She is very upset with your behavior."

"I'm not happy, Reverend Mother. I want to leave."

What sorrow on her face. *If only she could understand.* "Maybe for a while," I said. But I didn't mean that really. I needed to be free. *Don't cry; please don't cry.* I watched her, her mouth held tight and her eyes so sorrowful. I went to her and gave her a hug. "I'll be in touch," I said, but I didn't know when. I only knew that I would soon be free.

I went to the village phone box and phoned Ann. Between sobs, I asked her if I could stay with her for a few days. A gamut of thoughts and emotions whirled through my mind—guilt at leaving Sister St. Claire before she could find a replacement and sorrow for the pain I had caused my Reverend Mother—but still I wanted to stay the course I'd chosen.

"Mary, what's the matter?" Ann asked. I gave her a garbled version of my situation and without hesitation she said her husband would come and get me as soon as I was ready. I cycled back to the children's home. Sister St. Claire came out of the refectory with a scowl on her face.

"Reverend Mother called me," she said. "Don't you care? After all we've done for you." I had heard that from her many times, but usually it was, "after all *I've* done for you." I was too emotionally spent to talk. I walked up the wide staircase with its shiny banister and into my room. There I pulled out my case and started methodically packing.

Ann's husband came for me that evening. The children knew I was leaving and I could hear some of them crying as I walked down the passageway and closed the door behind me.

I stayed with Ann and her husband for a few days. In that time I did a job search and focused on things ahead. I checked out children's nurseries in and around the London area and soon secured a job in a nursery for babies and toddlers. Now I had freedom to do what I wanted. I continued my singing and dancing lessons, went to movie theaters and dance clubs with staff from the nursery, and felt determined to follow my dreams.

20

Mario

One evening, at the lively Café de Paris nightclub, I met Mario. Immediately smitten with his charm and his broken accent, I was swept off my feet—work and pursuit of a show business career faded into the recesses of my mind. For a while Mario wouldn't tell me where he worked. "Tell me," I'd say as I looked into his blue eyes, but instead he would plant a butterfly kiss on my mouth. Eventually he said, "For now I work as waiter. I have been to hotel school in Switzerland. When English improve, I go up." He meant he would be promoted. I loved the way he talked.

"You speak maybe German, French, Italian?" he had asked upon first meeting me. I just shook my head back and forth with a smile.

"No, only English," I said.

"You teach me English. I teach Italian, yes?" And he taught me words of endearment in his language: *amore, bacio, ti amo, bella,* and others. I loved everything about him—his smile, his teasing, his Italian suits and his good manners. He always opened doors for me and held his large black umbrella over us when it rained. Then one time we arranged to meet at Waterloo station and he was almost two hours late. I waited and fumed. Anger gave way to concern as I worried that something bad had happened to him. I was just about to leave when I saw him standing a few feet away. His smile melted my heart. He placed an imaginary kiss on the platform and bowled it toward me with his umbrella.

"You rascal," I laughed. "I was so worried." But relief at seeing him safe swept away my indignation.

I lived and dreamed Mario. We were together every spare minute. On one occasion as we dined in a little restaurant, he said, "You and I—we will marry." No argument ensued on my part and soon we visited the jeweler's shop for a ring.

We went to The Talk of the Town, an upscale nightclub in the heart of London, for our engagement dinner. Then we shared the news with a couple with whom I had been very close and whom Mario had also come to know. We decided to be married in a registry office with these friends as witnesses.

Starry-eyed, I flew to Paris with my husband—my first flight ever.

We sent our friends postcards telling them we were on our honeymoon. I marveled at the newness of all that I experienced. The children's home seemed a distant memory. I had entered a new and much more exciting world. We visited national monuments like the Eiffel Tower, the Louvre, the Arc de Triomphe, and other wonders of that city. One evening we went to the Sacre Coeur, a beautiful basilica built on Montmartre hill. Mario wanted to sit in on the service. We slipped into a pew and as the choir sang, Mario started to cry softly. Alarmed, I asked, "What is it Mario?"

"I'm remembering," he whispered. It made me think about the services in the chapel at The Home of Compassion. And a tear trickled down my face. We left and wended our way back to our hotel—where consumed with each other, our sorrow dissipated.

We settled in Surrey and started a family. Michael, a beautiful baby, grew into a talkative little toddler, and then I became pregnant with David. The children were our delight. Mario had a good job in a luxury resort complex. We phoned his Mama on occasions and I greeted her with the little Italian I knew.

I often talked to Mario about Reverend Mother and Sister St. Claire. During one of our chats, he said, "Why don't you call her?" I struggled as to whether I should or not. How would she receive me? Indeed, would she receive me? I had hurt her so badly. But in my heart I longed to be reunited. On a warm summer evening I made the call.

"My Mary! How are you my darling? Oh, do come and see me," she said. And I needed no second bidding.

We arranged to go as a family. We didn't have a car at that time and so we took the train from Motspur Park, where we then lived, to Thames Ditton. As gracious as ever, Reverend Mother received us. She shook hands heartily with Mario and then she and I embraced in a long and silent hug as I tried to stifle my sobs. She then turned her attention to the boys, and her eyes lit up. "What darlings," she said, "Oh my, what darlings."

Dorothy hovered in the background. She had prepared the table for tea. The familiar sight of thinly sliced brown bread and butter and wedges of fruit cake caught my eye; a plate of miniature jam tarts with a dab of cream in the middle of each completed the spread. Dorothy beamed at me and my heart filled with love for this faithful little maid who had served Reverend Mother for so long.

"How are you, Dorothy?"

"I'm well," she said, "Your boys are lovely." She looked at Reverend Mother. "Shall I make the tea, Reverend Muvver?" Dorothy still had no teeth.

We sat around the table. Mario gave eight-month-old David his bottle and I tussled a little with Michael, since he wanted to spread jam on his bread without any help. Reverend Mother laughed at that and said, "Let him try." Then she laughed some more as the jam got spread on the cloth as well. I sat at her table that day and I thought, *If I get any happier I'll burst!*

Reestablished with the only family I'd ever known, my world seemed complete. But there were more adventures in store; Mario had promised me that one day we would go to Italy. By the time our second son David had his first birthday a date had been set. Mario had bought the Berlitz self-teach guide and Michael sat next to me in our little sitting room as we learned the language for our eventful move. We repeated words after him: *buon giorno, buona notte la finestra, la porta,* and so on. Sometimes our little Mike rolled on the settee with laughter as he tried to roll his "rs." I listened and learned the melodic sounds that were like music to my ears.

We visited Reverend Mother frequently and I also went to the children's home to make my peace with Sister St. Claire. Reverend Mother loved the boys and I loved seeing her light up when we arrived. But our visits ceased when we finally left for Italy.

Mario had asked, "How would you like to go by boat and train?"

Crossing the English Channel didn't appeal to me. "Mario, I don't like boats, I'll get seasick," I said.

"Don't worry Bella, it's a short trip across the channel and then we'll be on the train and you'll like going through Switzerland, I promise." He hugged me. "*Ti amo,*" he whispered.

"*Anche Io,*" (I love you too) I said.

The highlight of our journey happened in Switzerland. Mario had booked a sleeper carriage, and with the steady rhythm of the train as it sped along, the boys were soon fast asleep. We woke up and readied ourselves for breakfast. The magnificent snow-capped mountains of Switzerland flanked both sides of the train. Mario laughed at my delight as I gaped in awe through the windows of the dining carriage. The chalets built on the mountainsides were so picturesque, many boasting huge planters filled with an abundance of colorful flowers. Feather mattresses hung over the balconies of those homes where the residents were already up and busy with their day.

Great excitement heralded our arrival. Mario's sister and her husband picked us up at the train station in Lugano. The family homes were just across the border in Varese, Italy. We were greeted and embraced with much enthusiasm and I did my best to absorb what they were saying. "*Che belli bambini,*" my sister-in-law said as she hugged the boys. She took thirteen-month-old Davy from me and planted kisses all over his face. Davy responded by crying loudly. I quickly rescued him. The family displayed much love. Every day we went to one of the four homes for dinner and every day the families from the other homes came bringing their contribution to the feast. I watched and listened to my three sisters-in-law and their husbands and my brother-in-law and his wife, their voices rising and falling as they talked and discussed with passion the issues of the day. Nephews and nieces ran here and there and as is the way with children, Michael joined them, with all seemingly unaware of the language barrier. *It's like a symphony,* I thought, *and Mama is the conductor!* She'd raise her voice above the cacophony of sound, bringing all into harmony as she directed us to sit around the table.

"*Ti piace* Mary?" (Do you like it?) she always asked as I tucked into the sumptuous fare, and I always said, "*Si Mama, molte bene.*"

Too soon, Mario had to leave for work. He had a job at the Grand Hotel Dei Castelli, which stood atop a peninsula jotting out into the Bay of Genoa. I missed him and he missed us. He found a little apartment in Sestri Levante, came to Varese and took us back to be with him there.

I took the boys for walks, pushing Davy in his stroller.

"*Buon giorno,*" people would say and always remark on my beautiful boys. It is the way of Italians to see all children as beautiful little darlings.

One day we were in a *pharmacia* buying baby formula. The *signora* insisted that I take some bibs and other baby items and I tried to explain to her that I didn't need them, but she kept saying, "*Regala.*"

"Mario, help," I called; he was in another part of the store.

The *signoria* with much gesturing excitedly talked to Mario.

He turned to me. "She wants you to have them as a gift, just because you're beautiful and our baby is beautiful," he said with a grin. Italy's charm and its people had assuredly captured my heart.

We returned to England for a short while and then in 1965, Mario secured a very good job in Freeport in the Bahamas, which meant a pleasant return for us to the sunshine we had come to love in Italy. Appointed as maitre d'hotel in the Rib Room, a high-end restaurant in the King's Inn complex, his hours at work were very long, but the monetary benefits excellent. The place hummed with tourists, mostly from America. The company provided accommodation for many of its staff and we had a large two-bedroom apartment. For two years Mario worked non-stop and was in desperate need of a break. We realized that even in constant sunshine and afternoon trips to the beach, a person still needed a vacation!

"You know what we'll do?" Mario said. "We'll fly to Jamaica for a few days. I'm not sure when, but soon." About a week later he came home late at night. "Can you be ready to fly to Jamaica in the morning?" he asked.

"I certainly can," I said as I hugged him. I packed a couple of suitcases. In the morning I went into the boys' room. "Who wants to go to Jamaica?" I said. I was six months pregnant at the time. We flew into a storm—a most terrifying experience. The huge plane plummeted, then rose. My four-year-old David looked at me with his big brown eyes and asked, "Are we going to crash, Mummy?" To which I replied, "Of course not Davy," as I tried to sound convincing. Once we landed and boarded a taxi for our hotel, I breathed a sigh of relief, but not for long—the cab driver drove as if we were being chased by a pack of wild dogs.

We stayed at the Casa Montego Hotel, rented a car to visit historical sites, enjoyed delicious meals, and listened to calypso music. It was similar to the atmosphere from the Bahamas where we lived, but for Mario there were no phone calls with issues that needed his attention, and it renewed him. Both boys enjoyed calypso. Davy got up and danced to the calypso music in the restaurant one evening and charmed the diners.

"Mummy," he said, "When I grow up I'm going to live in Jamaica forever."

Our vacation over, a quiet and uneventful flight took us back to Freeport.

A couple of months after our return I started having labor pains. We were in for a shock. I gave birth to premature twins. The fact that I was carrying two babies had gone undetected. Being six weeks premature, the poor little souls Daniela and Christopher had a rough start and the three of us in fact were touch and go for quite a while.

Mario and I attended a Methodist church on the Island and the first person to visit me was our minister. He called people in the congregation and asked them to pray for us.

The dire situation cast doubt on the survival of little Daniela. Both the babies were in incubators and weighed less than four pounds each. But Daniela had hyaline membrane disease, a condition resulting from a lack of surfactant in the lungs that caused the tiny alveoli to collapse with each breath she took. I had been heavily medicated and did not know about the situation until I woke up and saw Mario sobbing by my bedside.

"What is it Mario, we'll manage." I thought he might be overwhelmed with the news that we had twins. He pulled the chair close to my bedside and told me about Daniela.

"Dr. Taylor has asked another pediatrician for his opinion on treatment," he said, "a Dr. Kimmett from Canada."

We were interrupted by a knock on the door; a hand appeared holding a single red rose and then my obstetrician quickly entered the room. "Mary," he said, "don't you ever do that to me again!" It had been a very difficult delivery and a surprise one too. He placed the rose on my bed and said, "The babies are in good hands, we're going to believe they'll do fine."

Doctor Taylor came to explain Daniela's treatment; they planned to give her surfactant through a drip into the umbilicus.

On the third day he popped his head around my door and said with a big grin, "We made it!" Later in the morning I went home, but the babies had to stay. Mario ran between the hotel, home, and the hospital. He picked me up approximately every four hours and we'd go with Michael and David to see the twins.

One night I had the car and drove up to the hotel to get Mario. I said, "Let's skip the hospital tonight. I'm so tired and they're doing well."

"Are you sure?" Mario said, as he put his key in the lock. Then just as suddenly as I had said it, I changed my mind. For some reason I knew we had to go.

We reached the hospital and hurried down the corridor. For a moment, we froze, staring in disbelief through the nursery window. "No!" Mario screamed. Daniela lay blue and gasping, Mario grabbed the door, rushed in, and deftly opened the incubator and lifted her out. Her color quickly improved. We stood trembling with horror, realizing the oxygen supply had run out. There were no nurses anywhere. We ran around to the main area of the hospital and found a doctor doing rounds. "Come, please come," Mario urged as he grabbed his arm. The doctor saw our panic and followed us back to the nursery. A couple of the registered nurses came too; at the same time an elderly nurse slipped out of a side room. It turned out the regular nurse had phoned in sick and this elderly lady with no formal training had been called in as a replacement to watch over the babies.

The next morning Dr. Taylor's nurse phoned from his clinic. "Did you hear him?" she asked. "He was so angry. Just hold on—he wants to talk to you." What Dr. Taylor wanted to talk about revolved around the twins. He said, "I want you to get some friends together, scrub out your bedroom, remove carpeting, shoes—anything that can harbor bugs—and take the twins home. You'll have to keep the room at 80 degrees until they are stronger."

I had a close friend Kitty, a trained nurse. She became my greatest support and every day helped me feed the twins with eyedroppers. The babies progressed well. The first day they made little noises caused great excitement. Michael and David were at last allowed to peep in and see their tiny brother and sister.

However, the strain of all that had transpired took its toll and I became depressed, crying at the drop of a hat. My doctor diagnosed post partum depression and suggested to Mario that a change of scenery might benefit me. Abaco, one of the many Bahamian Islands, seemed an ideal setting. It had a resort and offered self-contained bungalows dotted between the palm trees. Arrangements were made for a Bahamian nanny to help me with the twins and we took the half-hour flight to Abaco one Sunday afternoon. Mario and the boys stayed overnight and returned to Freeport the next day. Mario's friend headed up the restaurant staff, and his wife kept me company, calling at my bungalow to accompany me to the restaurant for meals.

What a blessing our Bahamian nanny proved to be! She rocked the babies in her ample bosom and ceased their crying in no time. They continued to thrive and we returned to Freeport after a month. Daniela walked at ten months and Christopher the night before their first birthday.

"I really believe there is a God," Mario said, on the day they had started to thrive. And I believed with him.

Bahamian life brought much pleasure. Mario's job afforded him an excellent salary and he invested in the stock market. But over a period of time, a shift in government brought changes and uncertainty to the many expatriates who lived in the islands; even though the promise had been made not to kill the goose that had laid the golden egg—the goose slowly died. All the expertise that had secured tourism was now being squeezed out, work permits were refused and seemingly deliberate attempts were made to delay anyone getting renewals on time. So after five years of sandy beaches and sunshine, we returned to England by boat. I remember the blue sea changing to gray as each day brought us closer to Southampton.

In all our years away I had kept in touch with friends and of course written to Sister St. Claire and Reverend Mother. Their letters back were infrequent, but I knew they were getting on in years. Someone had written to tell me not to be disappointed, but Reverend Mother had become forgetful and that she would not know me. I left the children with Sister St. Claire and made my way to the Home of Compassion. Fear engaged me, fear at what I might see. I crossed the flagstone foyer and rounded the corner. There she stood at her door with a teapot in her hand.

"Reverend Mother," I said.

Recognition came instantly and the familiar smile lighted her face, "Mary, my Mary, where have you been, my darling?" Within seconds I embraced her as tears poured down my face.

From then on I visited her with my children every Saturday and stayed close to her over the months as her health started to fail—remembering always what had been.

My earliest photo

Reverend Mother

Victory party with the land army girls, with me second row from the bottom and Hazil in front and to my left, 1945

Outside "Newlands," our new home, with Hazil directly in front of me, 1948

St Agnes Children's Choir recording for a commercial, c. 1950

Me with Scruffy, 1951

Me at a garden party on the grounds
of the Home of Compassion, 1950s

Reverend Mother, Scruffy, and girls on
the grounds of the Home of Compassion

Garden party on the grounds of the Home of Compassion, 1950s

On the tennis courts, West London Hospital, with two med students, 1953

Nursing students, 1953

Bridesmaid at Ann's
wedding, 1955

Michael and David in Varese, Italy, 1963

At Sestri Levante, Italy, 1963

Michael and me in Switzerland, 1963

With David and Michael at Torquay, Devon, England, September 1964

Freeport, Bahamas, with David and Michael

Freeport, Bahamas–off to a wedding

Walking on the golf course with David, Freeport, Bahamas

In our apartment, Freeport, Bahamas, with David and the twins, 1970

The twins' second birthday, Freeport, Bahamas, 1970

Daughter-in-law Sue with Jasmine and Christian

With Al at Mike and Kelly's wedding, May 2002

Wedding day, June 22, 2002, with
my tall, distinguished man with the
silver-gray hair

Eldest son Mike escorts me down the
aisle after speaking to me firmly!

Me and Hazil on my
wedding day

Hazil as Matron of Honor and
son-in-law Jack as Best Man

Nancy and me on my wedding day

Al and me with Dave, Mike, Daniela, and Chris

Al and me with Kelsey, Jack, Dianne, and Annie

Dianne and Jack greeting guests at our wedding

With great-nephew Peter and his wife Addy, September 2003

With Daniela and son-in-law Mike on their wedding day, January 2004

Daniela and me on her wedding day

Patrice and Christopher

Mike and Kelly

Al and me on Family Vacation, 2005

Our two families on vacation in Collingwood, 2005

Kelsey and Mike, Family Vacation, 2005

The grandchildren – Christian, Annie, Jasmine, and Corbin

Great-nephew Reverend Peter Forrester with wife Addy, daughter Emily, and Peter Jr.

"Three brothers" – Dave, Chris, and Jack

Hazil with husband Jack, 2006

Close friends Ken and Maria Brooks

The littlest member of our family,
Baby Kyle, Mike and Daniela's son

Surprise 70th birthday party for me, with Hazil, Val, Priscilla, and Nancy

21

The Passing of an Era

One temperate day in the early seventies, with mild winds and periods of sunshine, Mr. Cattermole's fleet of cars slowly made its way out of the gravel driveway bearing the coffin of Reverend Mother. I sat in one of the cars with other adults who had grown up with me in the home. Red-eyed, I stared out as we slowly drove along High Street past St. Nicholas Church and past Boyle Farm cottage where we had lived prior to the war. The whole village had turned out to pay their last respects. The village policeman stood to attention and held his salute as we went by.

At the graveside I reflected on this gracious lady, the only mother I had ever known, who had decided at a moment's notice to take me into her Home of Compassion and how from that act of kindness she had expanded her ministry through the years to embrace children from all sorts of circumstances.

At that point Hazil came to mind. She had married at age seventeen in St. Nicholas church and I had been her bridesmaid. Sister St. Claire had made my dress and the dresses for the three little flower girls. It was a joyous day as we celebrated that new phase in Hazil's life. She now lived in Canada but our friendship remained strong.

With Reverend Mother's failing health and ultimate passing, the Home of Compassion saw much change. Some of the nuns had died while others had gone to live out their retirement years with their families. The private order of The Sisters of Mercy had come to an end, and from its conception in 1905 by its first Mother Superior to the death of my Reverend Mother, countless people young and old had benefited from its charity.

The Home of Compassion fell into the hands of a government run agency. The children's home closed and Sister St. Claire retired and moved into the Home of Compassion, where she died a few years later. Relatives of the few children who remained were consulted and alternate arrangements made for them.

The sunlight flitted through the trees in St. Nicholas graveyard as the vicar read the prayers. My mind strayed again. I thought of the serene gardens and lawns of the Home of Compassion on the other side of High Street where festive garden parties had been held every year to raise funds for the home. I thought of big name film stars who had come to open the fete and gave rousing endorsements to Reverend Mother and her work, and of the many supporters who set up tables to sell crafts, baked goods, and a variety of wares, cheerfully donating their proceeds at the end of the day. I thought of Sister St. Claire who had been in charge of the children's home all my life; I thought of her many talents and of her baked sponge cakes and fruit cakes—the best I ever tasted. I thought of her sewing skills, especially the exquisite smocked dresses she made. Her contribution to the fetes brought rich monetary rewards in the hundreds of pounds. Wealthy women in the surrounding areas came to buy her handmade dresses for their little girls and she often had advance orders with particular colors and patterns specified.

Then as a member of the St. Agnes Children's Choir, I had sung with my peers under the direction of our able music master who conducted our performances at the garden parties. And with excitement we had seen people gather at the tea tables as the announcement came over the speakers that the children were about to sing.

I thought of the River Thames that flowed past the bottom of the garden, of the people who strolled across the lawn during the garden parties to wave at boats cruising by toward Hampton Court Palace that stood on the opposite bank a little farther downstream.

The picturesque gardens and abundance of trees would soon be just a memory. I frowned remembering the times I had roamed the gardens and the poem I had written as a teenager to a particular tree that stood there:

Amid the grasses and the rushes, along the river's quietest part,
Stands a tree of noble splendor there I've placed my wondering
heart
Wonder why the secrets whispered to the river hurrying by
Are not whispered to me also, here I sit and wonder why.
Does the tree gently swaying tell of things long gone by?
Must I always try in vain to learn its secrets wonder why?
Is it just imagination does the river laugh at me?
And do I hear a mocking whisper from that tall and splendid
tree!

But now I had no reason to return to sit under that splendid tree—only perhaps to see Sister St. Claire now and then and to think about my dear Reverend Mother.

The memories of her funeral day—when I bid my final farewell to my mother and benefactor—are forever etched in my mind. I knew I was more than her adoptee. She had truly loved me and referred to me always as "My Mary."

22

Chaos

I busied myself in the narrow kitchen of our home, the year—1971. We had visited the family in Italy the previous year, but were now settled back in England and had bought a semi-detached house in a quiet cul-de-sac. It had been hard going. Much of our money had been lost in investments Mario had made in the Bahamas. But being resourceful and a hard worker, he soon secured steady work in a prestigious hotel in London.

We had enrolled the older boys, Michael and Davy, in school and initially I had stayed at home with the twins. But a day came when Mario expressed his concerns to me that funds were running low and that keeping the bills paid on time had become very difficult. He looked at me.

"I always vowed my wife would not work, but now I must ask you to see if you can find a part-time job," he said. I agreed, but realized difficulties lay ahead. I'd have to find work where the twins—at the time two and a half—could be accommodated. It happened soon enough. Tolworth Hospital had a nursery for the children of staff members. I faced challenges getting them up and ready each morning. We didn't have a car and it was particularly challenging on cold blustery mornings as I pushed them in their double stroller to the bus stop.

"I'll give you a hand love," a middle-aged woman had said, as the bus pulled up on that first morning.

"Here, give me one of the babies." And she lifted Christopher out while he eyed her suspiciously.

"It's all right Chrissie," I cooed, as I lifted Daniela.

"You get in," a man said, "I'll take care of the stroller." And that's the way it was on the days I went to work, with kind people helping me board the bus each morning.

I enjoyed work at the hospital and during lunch break I'd pop over to the nursery to see my twins. Over the next two to three years our status began to improve and we enjoyed friends and outings to parks and seaside vacations. Mario made improvements to the house and also the garden. He built a fishpond for the boys in the backyard.

Michael joined The Crusaders, a boys' club with a Christian focus. He relished club nights and made some good friends. David chose to take karate lessons, and at age 11 won the gold medal for intermediate boys division. How proud we were to sit in the audience as he stood on the podium to receive his award with Mario clicking away with the camera.

Because Mario worked in the hotel's restaurant, he tended to arrive home between midnight and 1:00 a.m. Subconsciously I'd listen for his key in the lock and settle down once I knew he had come home. One night I awoke with a start and tried to focus my eyes on the alarm clock. Two a.m.! I felt sick with worry.

"Where were you?" I demanded when he came in half an hour later. He gave me a half smile and said, "At a party with pretty girls." He went on to explain some students who were working at the hotel for the summer had received word they had passed their exams from their country of origin, and had invited him to join them in their celebrations.

"You could have phoned," I admonished.

"I'm sorry Bella, forgive me?" He called me Bella most of the time—a common Italian endearment meaning "beautiful." "Will you?" His blue eyes registered with mine and my heart warmed toward him. We hugged and I thought no more of it.

A few nights later Mario arrived home in the wee small hours and this pattern persisted over the weeks that followed. My worst fears were confirmed after several late arrivals when he finally said, "I've met someone, Mary." He didn't call me Bella and he didn't look at me. With this admission he stayed out late consistently, many times all night, coming in as I prepared to start the day after a sleepless night. Anger, betrayal, and desperation were my lot. I lost weight at an alarming rate.

"Mario, this can't go on," I told him.

"I'm so confused," he'd say. "I know I still love you but..." Then he'd ask me to give him a couple of weeks and he'd straighten everything out.

"What about seeing a counselor?" I pleaded in desperation. He surprised me by agreeing and I began to hope through this avenue we might get back on track. A social worker from the town social services came to the house once a week to counsel with us. Since Mario started work in the afternoons, we booked the sessions on my day off at 10 a.m. Talking everything through with this counselor seemed to help our communication and even Mario agreed the sessions had been worthwhile. Believing our marriage had been restored, the social worker terminated her visits—but it was not so.

The older boys knew about the situation and tensions were high in our home. Tempers were frayed and family life strained. I went to my doctor and asked for sleeping pills. I explained the situation and how the lack of sleep had affected my health. My doctor expressed anger at Mario and said, "Tell him to smarten up!"

To add to this upheaval, I developed a pain in my side that increased in intensity. A fibroid proved to be the cause and my doctor slated me for a hysterectomy. By this time the twins were attending kindergarten and I had transferred to the general hospital where I worked in gynecology, a very busy area with its own operating room and x-ray department. Not wanting to be nursed by my peers, I opted to have the surgery in a smaller hospital. The head surgeon from my own hospital performed the surgery and what should have been a simple procedure evolved into a nightmare. I woke up aware of several nurses and a doctor around my bed.

"Mary, can you hear me?" I moaned in response, "Why do I feel so out of it?"

"I've got a weak pulse," one of the nurses said. Much activity went on. I could feel someone setting up an intravenous drip, taking my blood pressure, and checking my pulse repeatedly.

"Mary," the doctor spoke again, "you've had a major bleed but I've got you stabilized." I heard him, but could not answer. Nurses removed the wet bedding, washed me down, and I floated off to sleep.

The next morning the head surgeon came to my bedside and told me he wanted me transferred to our own hospital. I had many battles to face on the road to recovery. Serious problems arose. My left lung collapsed, a retroperitoneal abscess formed in my right side and the team struggled to get me strong enough to go back to the operating room to have it incised. At this point Mario was told my chances of survival were fifty-fifty.

Friends came and gathered round my bedside. The twins had to go into foster care while Mario and the boys stayed in our home. He supervised the boys in the mornings, making sure they got off to school. On occasion, friends took the boys for a weekend. Mario continued working at the hotel, visiting me each day. Finally the team stabilized me enough to take me back to the operating theater and the abscess was incised.

Mario told me on one of his visits that his mama had taken ill and he had to go to Italy to see her. I believed this move involved his extramarital relationship that he seemed incapable of bringing to an end. The ward sister empathized with his story and promised they'd take good care of me and away he went to Varese, Italy, while friends took the boys into their home and the twins remained in foster care.

The days and nights dragged on. One night I spoke into the darkness of my room. "Oh, God let me die, let me die." With that my eyes were drawn to the doorway and I saw a light—a small light hovering—then it zigzagged to my bedside. I felt tremendous peace, my worries and cares dissolved, my pain left and as I drifted off into what I thought was eternity I whispered, "Thank You God, thank You."

Surprised beyond measure, I awoke the next morning and said to the staff-nurse who came into my room. "I am so hungry!" She fought back tears as she gave me a hug.

"Mary, that's the best thing I've heard in a long time." Although I had made that statement, when two nurses helped me walk slowly to the dining room, I could only manage a couple of bites. It took many days to gain any real appetite. I weighed 90 pounds and I knew in order to recover I had to eat. I tried, and after a time, the food became more palatable. I still needed therapy for my collapsed lung and daily dressings of my wound. In time I recovered enough to go to a convalescent home by the sea.

During the ordeal the children had visited. Sometimes the twins' social worker brought them to the hospital. I remember the day clearly when six year old Christopher told me, "You're going to get better Mummy, because I asked God." His pronouncement touched me. What had caused little Christopher to ask God?

We weren't going to church, although the schools at that time started the day with prayer. I thought about Christopher's remark and the appearance of the light and of my experience as a child in Manor Gardens. Did God really communicate with people?

23

Changes

"What do you think?" Mario spoke with enthusiasm, "We could make a fresh start in a new country." My husband had suggested that we apply for immigration to Canada. We were celebrating my homecoming from the convalescent home. He had ordered a cake with "Welcome Home Mummy" written on it in pink icing and as he sliced it up he shared this idea of emigrating.

"I'd like that," I said and besides, Hazil lived in Canada, in London, Ontario. Without a doubt I knew she'd agree to sponsor us. I relished the thought of seeing her again. She had visited in England and the Bahamas over the years and our friendship had never wavered. But now we could live in the same city.

Mario's affair had not yet come to an end, but he convinced me that a fresh start in a new country would keep the family intact and he promised to bring closure to that part of his life before leaving England. We got information about Canada and included the boys in the plans. Mario applied for work since he had to have a letter confirming employment before venturing out. The children were excited at the thought of flying to a new country. There were forms and more forms. A trip to Canada House cheered me when the official told me I would not be required to write my nursing exams again, since British trained nurses were recognized in the Commonwealth. Our applications for Canada accepted, we planned our next move.

We put the house on the market and it sold quickly; we had three months to pack up, sell off our goods, and get out of the house. My husband suggested that he should go first to find accommodation for us and get settled in his job. Fortunately, good friends helped me with the huge task of packing and selling off the furniture.

Other friends drove the children, Mario, and me to the airport for his departure. I had a sinking feeling in my stomach as I stood with him waiting for the boarding announcement. Something didn't seem right. He busied himself with the children and avoided eye contact, but then he looked at me and promised all would be well. The announcement came for his flight and he hurried away. I decided oversensitivity was my problem and driving back to the house with friends, I determined it would be fine just as Mario had assured.

In September 1975, I arrived at Toronto's Lester B. Pearson International Airport with the children. Mario was there to greet us, along with Hazil, Hazil's husband, and their two sons. They had come with two cars and we drove for two hours till we got to Hazil's home in London where she had prepared places to sleep and dinner for all of us. Hazil took me aside and said, "I think you should know that when Mario has been here visiting, a girl has been phoning to speak to him."

"Oh, no!" I said. I told Hazil what had been going on in our marriage and of Mario's promise of a new start. "Do you think the girl is in Canada or are they overseas calls?" I asked.

"Oh, no, she's calling from Oshawa, where Mario has been living. It's near Toronto."

Despair overtook me. I told Mario we needed to talk. He agreed and we walked around the block.

"Tell me Mario. Is it true your girlfriend is here in Canada?"
He didn't reply.

"It's true isn't it?" I cried, "Why, why? You promised me we were starting a new life."

"Listen," he said, "can you give me a couple of weeks and I'll have it all sorted out. The situation is temporary, I promise." I thought about the many incidents of our strained relationship, the late nights and the broken promises and the times before when he had asked for two more weeks. I knew our marriage had ended and I had to come to grips with it, yet I still hoped. We walked back to Hazil's house. The mealtime was tense. Mario hung around for a while, spent some time with the children and then said he had to get back to Oshawa that night. "I'll be in touch soon Bella," he said softly. He'd taken to using that endearment again. And then he left.

In a daze I struggled to focus my thoughts. I had four children and I couldn't stay at Hazil's house forever. I fluctuated between bouts of uncontrollable crying to periods of intense anger. Hazil's kindness and support sustained me. She housed me and the children for several weeks, took me to the school to register the children and advised me about the type of clothing the children would need for the winter ahead. The twins got quite excited when we went to buy snowsuits and boots. Hazil let me stay at her house until I pulled myself together. Not once did she suggest I should move on.

Slowly, as if coming out of a bad dream, reality took hold. After weeks of depression it dawned on me I had to act on what I knew I had to do—get on with life—not only for my sake, but also for the sake of the children. I walked into the house after seeing the children off to school.

"Hazil, I'm going to apply at the hospitals for work," I said. Determined, I sat down at the kitchen table and started that very day, unaware of a huge roadblock in my path. Contrary to the advice I had received on leaving England, each hospital to which I applied informed me that all overseas registered nurses were required to write the Canadian exams in order to practice. "What am I going to do?" I exclaimed.

"You could apply to Parkwood Hospital," Hazil volunteered. I knew she worked there as a nurse's aid and she thought maybe I could get a job in the same capacity. Parkwood specialized in geriatric care and focused on an aspect of nursing very different from the gynecological ward where I had worked in England. I hadn't planned to work in geriatrics but desperation born out of necessity urged me on and I applied. I didn't get accepted right away and only through persistent calls did the doors finally open for me to start work there.

I went to the bank to deposit my first paycheck into the joint account Mario had opened. Needing every penny in that account for the family, I spoke to the bank manager about my predicament and asked to have the funds transferred into an account in my name only and he kindly arranged it.

Next I determined to rent a house. "It's got to be in this subdivision," I said to Hazil. "Remember when we used to play 'mothers and fathers' and we always said we'd live next door to each other when we grew up?" Hazil laughed.

"Let's check the 'For rent' column," she said, spreading out the paper on the kitchen table. Together we pored over the paper concentrating on available homes nearby. As we did I sensed a lifting of my spirits. "Here's one," Hazil said, and she read out, "three bedroom town house with one and a half bathrooms."

I could manage the rent and decided to contact the landlord, until I noticed that the ad said to call after six p.m.

"I'm calling now," I said, even though the clock on the wall registered midday. A man answered the phone. "Are you the landlord for the house on Toulon Crescent?" I asked.

"Yes," he said.

"I want to rent it."

"Excuse me madam, but I have eight people who will be viewing the house tonight and tomorrow."

"I don't need to view it," I said. "When could I pay the first month's rent and when can I move in?"

The landlord taken aback, spluttered a bit, then said. "You want to rent without seeing?"

"Yes." I could hardly believe my own recklessness, but something seemed to be urging me on and I felt positive about the whole situation. After a few more exchanges and a tentative agreement made over the phone, we arranged to meet at three p.m. at the house on Toulon Crescent; I viewed the property and signed a rental agreement.

Hazil drove me to the mall and I shopped for furniture and other household items. The money in my account was barely enough to get us going. Hazil supplied us with many household items and soon we moved into our rented house. We were close enough that our children could run from one house to the other.

Some semblance of order started to take shape in my life although bouts of depression plagued me at times. The thought that Mario saw me as unattractive and that I was no longer his Bella tormented me. I'd fight back tears at this realization. But I discovered that other men found me attractive and some flirted with me in most extraordinary situations. I began to gain some confidence and my self-esteem became somewhat restored. Nevertheless, these incidents did not amount to anything and a big hole remained in my heart.

Winters in Canada were quite an experience. The second winter proved particularly harsh. I had to practically go mountaineering to make my way to the bus stop over mounds of snow piled up shoulder-high by the snow plough. The twins initially enjoyed the snow until one day Christopher with his glasses all steamed up trudged wearily into the house and announced, "Mummy I'm sick and tired of snow!"

I arrived at the hospital for the early morning shift one day and by eight a.m. a snowstorm had hit the city, paralyzing all transport and bringing everything to a standstill. Hospital staff blocked the phone lines as parents tried to locate their children. Eventually

I got through to our home and Mike answered the phone. "Oh, Mike I'm so glad you're there."

"Yes mother, he said, "I tried to leave, but the wind blew me back in!" The children had to fend for themselves that day and all night, since no one could go anywhere.

Staff at the hospital did double shifts. Mattresses were placed in the auditorium, bathtubs, armchairs, and even the dentist chair served as makeshift sleeping spots for whenever a soul could take a break. Nancy, one of the nurses I had become great friends with, paired up with me to work one of the shifts, and we found ourselves bursting into fits of hilarity, no doubt the result of our overtiredness.

My life went on without Mario. At first he stayed away for a few months, then one day he showed up on my doorstep. *Is he coming home?* I wondered, but no. He had just come for a visit. Nevertheless the children were happy to see him and we went to the park as a family. He continued to visit occasionally and in the winter taught the twins to ski. I always wanted to know if he had anything new to tell me, especially about the prospects for a renewed life together. But his life in Oshawa had a strong pull on him. The separation took its toll on all of us and the children demonstrated typical behavioral problems caused by family breakup. There was nothing to do but keep going and Hazil proved to be a tremendous help and support.

I made friends at the hospital, and chummed with a nurse who lived in the same subdivision as me. If Hazil and I were not working the same hours, I often got a ride with Lynn. Sometimes Lynn came in for a tea before going home. On one occasion she sat looking thoughtfully at the twins as they played. "It's a shame for them to be without their daddy," she said. Then she looked at me and asked, "Has it ever dawned on you that what's happening with your husband could be spiritual?" I knew Lynn to be a devout Catholic. I sat and mulled over what she had said, then asked, "What exactly do you mean?"

"Let me ask you this. Do you believe in God?" she inquired.

Instantly my mind flashed back to a lecture I had attended in England just a few weeks before leaving for Canada. The title of that lecture had piqued the curiosity of doctors, nurses, and others—'Spiritual Warfare: Real or Imagined?' I remember we finished our duties and left a skeleton staff to handle the wards. When I entered the room with another colleague, the packed auditorium gave us no alternative but to stand at the back. Four doctors presented that day and each one gave information of a patient in their care who had demonstrated behavior that terrified those that loved them, the upshot being that prayer had been the answer to their problems. One of those stories remains with me to this day—the story of a teenage girl from a wealthy family. A doctor told how these parents had two children—the girl and a younger brother. One summer the girl got involved with Hell's Angels bikers; her behavior went from bad to worse and no amount of medical consultation or prescribed antipsychotic drugs helped. She dyed her hair black, wore black lipstick, black fingernails and heavy black eye makeup. Her parents finally went to this doctor and said, "We think our daughter's problem is spiritual." The relieved doctor shared with them that he thought so too and offered to contact the pastor of a church in the area for help. Halting now and then to compose himself as he shared with us, the doctor told how the pastor, deacons, and members of the congregation had prayed for the girl and how she, after two or three hours of prayer, had been restored to her right mind. That doctor said he compared it to the Bible stories about Jesus.

A hushed silence followed the doctor's comments. The presentation over, we returned to our wards. I heard a variety of remarks. Some said, "It gave us something to think about," and others scoffed. I tucked it in the back of my mind, but now Lynn's question brought it to the fore.

"Lynn," I said excitedly, "maybe if I pray, Mario will come home. A couple of days ago someone from a church nearby came to my door with a brochure. I'm going to phone the pastor and ask him if he knows anything about spiritual battles."

I rummaged through the kitchen drawer, found the brochure, dialed the church number, and then handed the brochure to Lynn while I waited for an answer. The kindly secretary told me the pastor was out doing prison ministry. *Prison ministry,* I thought, *what did that mean?* "Would you like someone else to visit you, one of the deacons, perhaps?"

"Look I don't want to be rude, but for some reason I want to talk to your pastor. I'm really not sure why," I finished lamely. The secretary reassured me and promised the pastor would come to see me as soon as he could.

That same day Hazil came to the house and our children played outside. Lynn had stayed for supper and the three of us were drinking tea. The pastor phoned and asked if it would be convenient to visit. I agreed, eager to get my question answered. He arrived within ten minutes of the call.

A pleasant young man, he invited me to pose my question and I did. I explained that Mario had left me and the discussion with Lynn had led me to seek answers. Did he think if I prayed God would bring Mario back? He surprised me with his response, not exactly dismissing my questions about spiritual warfare or praying, but focusing more on God and His Son Jesus. Like Lynn, he said, "Do you believe in God?" It astounded me that I hesitated to answer. I thought of Reverend Mother and her life—one devoted to God. She had believed! But I thought of God as being faraway and remote. Then I started remembering again those seemingly inexplicable experiences I'd had in the woods as a child and of the time in my hospital bed when I asked God to let me die and instead, the light came giving me peace. Had they been spiritual? Could it have been God?

To his question, I said, "I'm not sure." The pastor spoke again. "There is a Scripture in the Bible that tells us all are sinners and fall short of God's glory. In order to make ourselves right with God, to be reconciled to Him, we have to say we are sorry, confess our wrongdoing, and ask for forgiveness. Basically, man has separated himself from God, refused to follow His laws and of course this is why problems persist in the world."

It irked me that he said we were all sinners and I challenged him on that.

"Are you telling me I'm a sinner? I've been a good wife and mother. Mario is the one who left."

"That is true," he said, "but everyone sins. For instance, could you honestly say to me that you've never done anything wrong?" Still feeling slightly rattled, I realized I could probably produce quite a list.

"No I couldn't."

The pastor explained that Jesus had actually died on the cross for me and every other human being on the face of the earth. Then he said, "If you're willing to confess your sins, and I don't mean list them off one by one, because Jesus knows about them already, but tell Him you're sorry and ask Him to come into your life, He will and He'll help you."

I hesitated and then said, "This all sounds a bit far-fetched to me. I think I'm a 'doubting Thomas.'" Patiently he shared more, telling me that God had already revealed Himself to me in many ways and that it may also have been God who had motivated my call to the church.

"There's a prayer you can pray right now and I promise you if you do God will reveal Himself to you, on one condition—that you pray it with sincerity."

"What is it?" I asked.

"Just as I told you, confess, ask forgiveness, and ask Him into your heart. Would you like to ask Him now?"

"Well I suppose I've nothing to lose," I said.

He took both my hands and bowed his head. "Mary, when you say this prayer—believe with all your heart that Jesus, God's Son, will hear it."

"Why Jesus?"

"Because nobody can come to God, but through Jesus, He is our intercessor. He is the one who takes our prayers to Father God."

I hesitated again and then said, "I'll do it." I repeated the simple little prayer after him. "Dear Lord Jesus, please come into my life, my heart, and forgive me of my sins. Thank You for dying on the cross for me. Amen." Then the pastor prayed for me, asking God to help me through the days ahead. We exchanged a few more words and he told me about the importance of attending church. "One of our church buses comes into your subdivision on Sundays," he said. "I'll ask the driver to call for you." As he left, I said, "You won't forget about the bus will you?"

24

Green Pastures

The deafening noise continued unabated. Children laughed, shouted and chattered to one another as the bus made its way through the subdivision. Kevin stopped the bus every so often to pick up more children as his soft-spoken fiancée, Cathy, did her best to keep the children in order, especially the boys who seemed bent on seeing who could shout the loudest!

I sat on the bus with my children, most of the time gazing out of the window with a silly grin on my face. It had been four weeks since the pastor of Royal View Pentecostal Church had come to my home. I couldn't believe the change in me. Depression had been replaced with joy, despair with hope, and fear with assurance. All my life I had believed in God, but had never understood, or even been told about the personal relationship one could have with Him through His Son Jesus. I thought of the friendships being forged at the hospital and of my neighbors. I would have to tell them about the little prayer that made the difference. Truly amazing!

The bus pulled into the church parking lot and the children, including mine, tumbled out and made their way to the classrooms. I attended beginners' class, where an overview of the Bible and its message was taught; and at home I read the Bible at every opportunity, not because I had to, but because I wanted to.

"Good morning, Mary. How are you?" Betty, a vibrant woman standing at the entranceway, asked the question.

"I'm fine thanks." The cheerful friendliness of the people at the church resonated with me. People greeted each other with hugs and handshakes and asked after members who were sick or had some problem. For every difficulty, they promised to pray. *It's like the nun in my training hospital in England,* I thought, *she always said she'd pray for me.*

Every week I received a letter from the pastor encouraging me in my newfound faith. He called me one day to say he would be away for two weeks and if I needed any help during his absence, the substitute pastor would be available. In an evening service upon his return, after lively singing of hymns and choruses, and a thought provoking sermon about Jesus' love for all mankind, he invited people to go to the altar to pray—a frequent occurrence in the church. I always went forward. I'd ask God to let Mario know about Jesus and I believed with all my heart that eventually he would.

"Oh, Lord," I heard Betty saying, as she stood beside me with her hand on my shoulder. "You see us here and you see Mary asking for her husband. Please let him know You as we do." A man's voice took over; I felt his hand on my other shoulder. I heard his voice break as he talked to God about Mario. Then, sensing that something unusual was occurring, I became afraid.

"God," I whispered, "If you're real, give me a sign." Immediately my head came up and I looked at the pastor. Tears were streaming down his face and he prayed in a language I didn't understand. Before I had time to take it all in, I felt as if shafts of brilliant light were pouring into the depths of my soul, shafts accompanied by inexpressible love. I turned to Betty, "God's real," I said, "God's real," as tears of unmitigated joy ran down my cheeks.

"Bless you," she said as she hugged me. "Of course He's real." The service finished with the whole congregation singing at the top of their voices, *"Because He Lives."*

The following day at the hospital as I went about my duties, I had to look down to see if my feet were touching the floor. When I looked out of the window it seemed I had never seen the sky so blue or the grass so green! I managed my work assignments and had time to help other nurses on the unit. That's how I developed a friendship with Priscilla. Toward the end of the shift we often worked together assisting patients to the washroom and getting them ready for therapy. I had told Priscilla about Mario. "How can you be so happy all the time when your husband's left you?" she asked me one day. And I told her. She couldn't get enough of hearing about Jesus.

I explained about the little prayer that I'd prayed. "It's unbelievable when you think of all the people who believe in God, but they don't have this personal relationship, because no one's told them," I said to Priscilla, as we walked down to the cafeteria. We got our food and went to a table.

"Can I join you guys?" It was Lynn.

"Sure," I said.

"Are you still going to that church?" Lynn asked.

"Yes and I am learning so much, I've entered a whole new world."

"Can I come into your world too?" Lynn said with a grin. We all laughed.

I turned to Priscilla. "Remember that book I told you about, *Run, Baby, Run?*" She nodded. "That guy's in town tonight speaking at a church. Do you want to come and hear him?"

"Are you kidding? I'd love to."

I turned to Lynn. "Want to come?"

"Tell me more," she said.

I explained how Nicky Cruz, had been a street gangster and how God had told a pastor by the name of David Wilkerson to go to New York and tell the members of the gangs about Jesus. Lynn cocked an eyebrow. "So I continued, "Nicky Cruz prayed the same prayer I prayed and now he's a pastor."

"Okay I'm coming," Lynn said.

The children stayed with Hazil that night and Priscilla and Lynn, after listening to Nicky, went to the front of the church and prayed the prayer. Sometimes after that Lynn would come to our church to take in an evening service. She said there were similarities to the charismatic services she attended in her own church. But we all grew in our faith.

Hazil came to the church and she prayed the prayer, but eventually she returned to her Anglican roots and of course it didn't matter as long as we all knew about the prayer that made the difference.

As summer approached, the pastor placed information in the church bulletin about a Christian camp in Paris, Ontario, about one hour away. Betty told me she always went and she encouraged me to go too. "The camp offers a variety of activities for the children and adults alike and the rates for a cabin are very reasonable," she said. "There's only one drawback—people mostly book a year in advance, but sometimes there are cancellations so give it a try. I'll pray that God has something for you. Call at ten in the morning, that is the time the secretary, Mrs. Shields, goes to her office."

I stored this information in my mind. Around 7:30 a.m. on Monday morning I busied myself cleaning up the children's rooms and preparing breakfast. *Call now!* Where had that thought come from? *Could this be Jesus?* With excitement and perhaps a little apprehension, I dialed the number.

"Hello. Mrs. Shields. Can I help you?"

"I'm calling to see whether you have a cabin for family week? It would be for me and my three youngest children."

"Well my dear," she said, "someone has just canceled their accommodation for that very time slot. I can book you right now if you like." Hardly able to contain myself, I gave the necessary information to Mrs. Shields, hung up, and phoned Betty to tell her what had happened.

"Praise God," Betty exclaimed. It was a phrase I came to hear many times and one I came to utter myself with much sincerity in answer to my many prayers.

That summer we went to Paris, Ontario, to Braeside Christian Camp. I had never been camping in my life. I entered the cabin; what a culture shock! Cobwebs hung from the rafters like worn out lace and creepy crawlies were up there too! No wonder Betty told me to bring cleaning items. My children ran off to explore the camp grounds and find kids they knew from the church while I stood staring in horror at four roughly hewn bunk beds and more than a few big bugs flying around in the rafters.

"Hello Mary." Betty came into the cabin accompanied by Maud, another lady from our church.

"Betty this is terrible," I wailed, "I can't stay here."

I saw Maud raise her eyebrows then give a little smile. "You know something; our Jesus was born in a manger."

"I know, but it doesn't help," I grumbled.

"I'll help you clean up," Betty said, "once that's done you'll be surprised at how cozy it will be."

That did it. I determined not to complain anymore. We went to work cleaning and as the days went by the cabin seemed homier and I more content. There were several pastors and speakers from the U.S. at camp and I attended as many sessions as I could. My children went to the children's church and activities, and in a glorious evening service, I felt the presence of the Holy Spirit come into my life.

When we returned home, I joined our church choir and the following year we sang at the camp. Church members enjoyed every aspect of church life and the choir practices were no exception. We practiced on Wednesday nights while the children went to their various activities. Priscilla attended the church now and her rich alto voice was an asset to the choir. Then Betty, Priscilla, and I formed a trio and sang in our church and out in the community.

We practiced in my home, but my children did not stand on the cheering line—they thought our music old fashioned! Even so we sang in seniors' homes and other churches.

Later on I asked the pastor what he thought about me hosting a monthly women's prayer meeting in my home and he supported the idea. Prayer meant talking to God about our troubles and other people's troubles, our dreams and their dreams, and our desires and their desires. We told Him about loved ones that we hoped would know Him like we did. We prayed for many people who never knew we prayed for them and then down the road we'd see the prayers answered.

In this period of time, I worked as a relief nurse. This meant being called in to work any shift, anywhere and anytime. A summons to the office of Miss Hazelwood, the nurse administrator, had me concerned. A gentle pleasant lady, she asked me to sit down. "Mary it's been brought to my attention that you have refused to work Sunday shifts several times. Would you care to explain why?" I think God must have been laughing as I went on and on about my faith and how I couldn't possibly miss church. I stopped, aware that she understood—in fact she positively beamed. "I believe too," she said. "Even so, God still wants us to care for the sick; we can't abandon them because it's Sunday." I left the office thrilled to know Miss Hazelwood had prayed the prayer that made the difference. I was disappointed that I'd have to work on a Sunday, but I knew in my heart she was right.

Mario came to the church once or twice and the pastor showed him a great deal of kindness. Once he sat in the pew weeping, but he couldn't bring himself to go forward and pray to God. I still believed he would come back to us. But eventually a sheriff arrived at my door with divorce papers. I cried and at first refused to take the package. The sheriff said, "I'm sorry ma'am, but you have to sign for it," and tearfully I did.

Had God let me down? Four people had given me a verse from the Bible over the previous month. Priscilla had written it on a slip of paper and passed it to me in church, two sisters had written it on the bottom of a card they'd sent me in the mail and Hazil stopped her house cleaning one day called me on the phone and said, "I'm not sure where the Scripture is, but I think you're supposed to read it. It starts off with, 'Fear not and be not afraid.'"

"You're the fourth person to give me that Scripture," I said with excitement. "It must mean Mario's coming home."

That day I read the Scripture again. It said that God was with me, that He would help me and take care of me. It didn't make any reference to anyone else. I realized then that God doesn't make people do anything; He waits for them to come to Him.

The days passed by and the children continued to face difficulties. At fifteen, Michael decided he wanted to go back to England and he did return for a summer. David struggled with every aspect of his new life. He frequently opted out of school and eventually stopped going altogether. I'd come home from work to find him still in bed.

Again I sought professional help—this time not for my marriage, but for my children. A social worker insisted the whole family attend the sessions. She invited us to sit down. Chairs were placed here and there around the room, but we chose to sit in close proximity on one settee.

The sessions didn't help and David refused to go to school and became quiet and withdrawn. The sad part was that he had done so well in his last term in England the same year that he had won his gold medal in karate.

Christopher's teacher called me to discuss his behavior. In contrast to his brother, he was full of confidence and unrestrained energy. Unfortunately, he disturbed the class by getting up and walking around and once doing handstands against the wall much to his sister's embarrassment. However, his teacher, who confessed to me that she just loved him, decided to put his desk next to hers where she could keep a closer eye on him. And that did help.

Daniela decided one day that she wanted to run away. Hazil and I had taken the children to the mall and as we walked to the entrance we realized Daniela was missing. After at least a half-hour of frantic searching we found her crouched behind one of those huge garbage containers. She couldn't explain why she had run off. I hugged her and told her I loved her and to stay close.

The children did eventually settle to a degree and we established a routine that included church activities.

Mario's support payments were not always forthcoming and we had some bare bones experiences. It was humbling on our first Christmas to receive a huge amount of groceries from the church including a turkey.

Nevertheless, I absolutely believed that God must be directing people to help us. On one occasion, the weekend loomed and the support money had not come. I talked to God about it. I said, "Jesus you see that we need groceries; please could the money come before the weekend?" Friday came but no money. I refused to be downhearted, believing God would come through for us—and He did. The pastor's wife called me late Friday evening telling me she would pick me up at 9:00 a.m. the next morning. "We're going grocery shopping and you're to pick up everything you need and I'll pay for it," she announced.

"Thank you God," I shouted as I hung up the phone. "You're just too much!"

25

Election and Betrayal

"Hello, Mary speaking." I tucked the phone to my shoulder and tilted my head as I peeled potatoes.

"It's your pastor, Mary. How are you?"

"Good, thank you, pastor."

"Mary the reason I'm calling is to let you know you've been nominated to be president of the women's ministries. Now you should know two other ladies have also been nominated but I recommend that you let your name stand. You've come along by leaps and bounds over the last year and we," he said, meaning the board, "see you have leadership qualities."

"Oh, dear," I said, alarmed at such news. Without a doubt I had grown by leaps and bounds regarding my knowledge of God. And somehow, the absolute certainty of believing had made me quite open to telling others. Many nurses had come to believe as I did—had prayed the prayer and were full of enthusiasm too, but president of women's ministries? Leading some 80 to 90 women, organizing monthly events, along with an executive—*all a little daunting*, I thought. And then getting up in front of the whole congregation to make announcements—I just felt I couldn't.

"Mary."

"Yes Pastor. I really don't think I could do this," I stammered nervously. The pastor pointed out that once a person knew God, He—God—helped one to achieve.

"Well, if I agree to let my name stand and I get elected will someone help me—show me the ropes?"

"Of course, my wife always sits in on the committee meetings and gives direction if needed."

"All right, Pastor," I said. "I'll let my name stand." And before I had time to mull it over for any length of time, I had the job of president.

I threw myself with enthusiasm into the role and when I made my first announcement, I hoped the congregation couldn't hear my knees knocking! The ministry encompassed many facets of Christian life, and in my role I arranged speakers, special events, and different themes for each month. Not to say I did this alone—there were women far more competent than me to take the lead in flower arranging, craft activities, and food preparation. And the pastor's wife proved to be a tremendous support.

Along with these activities, I continued working at the hospital and eventually told my head nurse I had decided to study for my nursing registration. "About time," she said.

It proved to be a challenge. First I had to take a leave of absence from the hospital; then I applied for some financial support from the government and got $450.00 a month. Various people helped with the children. At the end of the year, I wrote my exams and returned to the hospital as a registered nurse. With my first pay check, I grocery shopped as I hadn't done in a long time. When David saw the full fridge, he said, "Boy, Mum, we should take a photo of this!"

During one of my study sessions out of town, I had asked a couple from the church with children of their own if they could take the twins. After some deliberation they consented. I felt confident that a stable family environment would be a good situation for them. But tragically, during this period, Greg Newcombe, the man of the household, molested my ten-year-old daughter. Daniela didn't tell me about it until years later when she was in her late teens.

By then, Daniela was studying at Humber College in Toronto. During spring break she had come home, and one afternoon during her stay we visited my friend Pat who lived down the road. That same afternoon, Greg's fourteen-year-old niece Francine visited Pat and her daughter. Their friendship went way back. Eleven-year-old Francine and her family, along with the Newcombes, had all moved from London at the same time to the same city and attended the same church.

The visit and chit-chat at Pat's house over, my daughter and I left.

"Do you want to drive?" I asked as we walked to my car.

"Sure, Mom."

As Daniela put the key in the ignition, I said, "My goodness, I wonder what happened to Francine; she is so changed from when we saw her three years ago." Daniela froze, gripped the steering wheel and let out a piercing scream.

"He's doing it to her, he's doing it to her," she sobbed, over and over again.

Startled at such an outburst I could only ask, "Daniela, who's doing what? Tell me!" Between uncontrollable sobs, she shared what Greg Newcombe had done to her as a little girl. I listened in disbelief then found myself sobbing along with my daughter as we rocked together in my car. Grief gave way to fury. I looked up.

"I promise you Daniela," I said blowing my nose, "I will take action tomorrow." And I did. I called the pastor of the church. By this time my first pastor had moved on to another pastorate, but I told the incumbent what had transpired and I told him I planned to call the authorities—the Children's Aid Society—after I'd finished talking with him. The pastor said he would contact the church that Greg now attended. He did so and the man admitted he had sexually abused my daughter.

The CAS was sympathetic—they took the details and acted on what I told them. Not only that, they kept me informed and let me know how the investigation progressed. Realizing that he had a serious problem, Greg agreed to go for counseling sessions.

I anguished for Daniela, and in some ways, for myself also as all the horrible memories of the abuse I had endured at a similar age came rushing back. It seemed impossible that she should have suffered the same fate, especially since she had been left in the care of those I had thought were trustworthy friends, not to mention active church members.

Daniela didn't want to press charges. "I just want Francine to be okay Mom," she said. I respected her decision; even so, for myself I wished she had brought charges so that at least she might have some closure for herself—the victim.

My sons learned about the abuse and they were furious. Over a period of time, along with their sister, they stopped attending church. "Mom, I don't know how you can still go to church," David shouted. His eyes blazed with anger as he banged his fist on the table.

"But David, it wasn't God. It was that Newcombe fellow; he's the one who did it."

"Don't say that Mom. If God's supposed to be all loving and all knowing, how could He let such things happen to Daniela?"

David had a point. *Oh God why, why did it happen to Daniela and to me too?* I knew that God was real, but I didn't have all the answers. I understood that each person has a free will and that each is still free to do right or to do wrong. People make choices and those choices have consequences—for themselves and others.

I grieved for my children and all they were suffering through but I could not turn my back on the God who had become so real to me. He had helped me and directed me through so much. He had given me such inner peace during what could have been times of torment. I prayed for my children and asked God to touch their hearts and show them His love.

During earlier years when the children were still attending the church, an idea came to me that I should launch a ministry for single parents and their children. The idea was triggered when I found a little drawing that Daniela had done. She had drawn a picture of herself and Christopher with a little caption near each of them, one read, "I wish my daddy would come back" and the other said, "So do I." Then below that a round face with the mouth wide open and tears spilling out of the eyes, with the caption, "Daddy come back." Out of this, Single Heart Ministries was birthed. After some discussion with the pastor regarding the need for such a ministry, a committee quickly came together and we determined that our focus would not only be to single parents, but to the children in single parent homes. The ministry thrived. Single fellowship Bible studies were well attended. And every last Saturday of the month we all met at the church with our picnic lunches and ventured forth with the kids. We went to the beach, conservation areas, parks, museums, and fossil hunting to name but a few of our activities. And every January, we had a wonderful get together at the home of Bob, a single dad with five children. The kids and some of the adults played ice hockey or skated on the pond nearby and once the outdoor activities were done, we'd all congregate in Bob's house to watch fun videos, play board games, and eat good food. Now the single adults and their children had their own group and a place within the church family.

Although our group bonded together, still for each one we longed for what we once had—a spouse. I know for me a void remained. The stance of the church at that time was that divorced people could not remarry. It remained a hotly debated issue for many of us. My friend Nancy, whose marriage had broken up, brought up the topic one day as we sat at my dining table sipping tea. Nancy had prayed the prayer one night when attending a Christian rally to which Priscilla had invited her.

"I can't see why a loving God would punish me for someone else's wrong doing," I said.

"No," Nancy agreed, "we know we're not perfect and never will be on this earth, but why would our heavenly Father hold us responsible for someone else's behavior?"

"I don't know. It's a quandary," I said with a laugh, "but He sure is keeping me busy and maybe that busyness will take the place of a husband."

"At least for now," I added as an afterthought.

26

Friends

I waited for Dianne to take my phone call. Her secretary told me she'd be with me momentarily. I waited and reflected on how I'd met Dianne. Friends were at my home for a prayer meeting and I had told them about the delivery of my divorce papers. "I wish I could find a good lawyer," I said. "Someone who believes as I do."

"I know of one and she's great," one of my friends informed me. And so I had called to make an appointment and she had taken care of my legal issues with much sensitivity and care. Now I was approaching her for an entirely different reason.

"Sorry to keep you waiting. How are you, Mary?" Dianne's voice interrupted my musing.

"Very busy, but very well, thank you. I was calling to ask if you might speak to our women's group either this month or next?"

Dianne readily agreed and a date was set. She came to our church and spoke to a full house. At the end of the evening she told me about her parents and how they had started a Christian retreat center called Gilead in the countryside about an hour's drive out of London. "You might like to consider it for a ladies retreat sometime," she said and she gave me the phone number.

At our next executive meeting, I told the ladies about the Christian retreat center. I had contacted Dianne's parents, Allan and

Fran Haskett, for details in advance and brought the information to the table. The enthusiasm for a retreat couldn't have been greater and within a couple of months we had the sign-up sheet full for an overnight getaway that became the first of many retreats we would have at Gilead through the years, eventually including day retreats for Single Heart Ministries too. The groups walked the beautiful trails and savored the tranquility there.

For me a long friendship began with Allan and Fran Haskett. Once my children were grown, I often went out to Gilead to spend a couple of days with them to walk the trails and to take in the beauty of God's creation.

"Tell me about your family, Mary," Fran had said one time. We were sitting in the breakfast nook waiting for Al to come in from the yard. She knew already that I was a single mom, that I worked as a nurse, and that I was actively involved in the church, but she wanted to know more about my life and my background. She showed a genuine interest. I told her what little I knew of my natural mother and how Reverend Mother had adopted me.

"Did you ever try to find your family?"

"Once long ago in England, the Salvation Army found my mother but they sent me a letter to the effect that my appearance would be stressful for her family and I should think carefully before going any further. I decided at that point not to pursue it."

By this time Al had joined us. "You have a right to know," he said, "have you thought about trying again?"

"I really haven't, but maybe I should. I'll have to give it some thought."

I drove home that day with the conversation I'd had with Al and Fran playing over in my mind and especially my last comment—*I'll have to give it some thought.*

And I thought about Hazil—how she had found her mother a few years before and received a cool reception. She had even been to the Isle-of-Wight to meet her mother, who told her she would

introduce her as a friend and no one must know the real relationship. But much later a change had occurred when Hazil decided to
pursue a family search on her father's side and through this connected with her brother. Before this contact, he had no idea that
she even existed. I remember well his visit to Canada to meet Hazil.
He totally accepted her as his sister and included me in their plans
for a day trip to the beautiful Elora Gorge, where we enjoyed lunch
in the Old Mill restaurant overlooking the falls.

With such a great reception by her brother, she then communi-
cated with cousins on the Isle-of-Wight who shared with her an exten-
sive family tree of which she was now a welcome part. Hazil and her
brother now alternate visits between England and Canada on a regular
basis. She has been royally treated by aunts and cousins—her mother's
rejection of no consequence in light of the passage of time.

I drove on, my mind going back even further to the St. Agnes
Home for Children during the time that I had worked there at Reverend Mother's request after passing my exams. She had phoned
me one day and asked me to come and see her at the Home of
Compassion. I smiled at the recollection. When I walked into her
room, she greeted me warmly.

"Come darling. This is my Mary," she said to two men who
jumped up and enthusiastically shook my hand.

"Sit down, Mary and these gentlemen will explain."

The gentlemen were newspapermen and they wanted to write
a story about me for the Evening Standard, a national paper, and
take photos of me at the children's home. *Oh, my goodness,* I thought,
all England's going to know about me! And all England did; letters
poured in by the hundreds, saying how touched they were by my
story and how they admired me for helping Reverend Mother after
all she had done for me. Not only that, many sent donations. One
note mystified and excited me. I have it to this day. It was written
by someone who knew of me since my birth and had sent it anony-
mously. Could it have been my mother, or her husband, who had

visited me as a baby? The note read: "*Dear Mary, Glad to know you have found happiness. Keep on that lovely smile. You will find more happiness later in life. I will always think of you and pray for you. Bless you.*"

God only knows who wrote that note and I'm sure I will meet the writer when I get to heaven.

27

A Revelation

March 1976 was the month the pastor of Royal View Church had explained to me about the prayer. Now some 20 years later, with my children having left the nest, the wonder of it had not dimmed. I continued to be involved in my church and helped out in many areas. I tried at all times to be a representative of the Lord Jesus Christ, showing kindness and consideration in whatever situation I found myself. Sometimes I faced difficulties at work, but I counted these happenings as a test. Could I hold steady in difficult circumstances? Could I represent the love of Christ? Sometimes I failed, but I tried my best and if I felt I needed to put something right with a colleague, I did so.

One Wednesday evening after Bible study I met Hans as I walked across the church foyer. Hans and his wife impressed me with their gentle ways, they were regular attendees and involved in ministries in the church.

"Hello Mary," Hans said, "could I have a word with you?"

"Yes," I said, eyeing him with caution, mainly because I didn't feel I could handle any more commitments. Hans smiled.

"I've been talking to Pastor Fess; we are looking for people who would be willing to take a course that is currently being offered at London Gospel Temple."

"Yes," I said, slowly.

"The course is called Ancient Paths and helps people to work through hurts from their past."

"Yes," I said for the third time. We both laughed.

"Would you be interested in taking the course? We would like to build a team of people who could later facilitate the course at Royal View, but in order to do that you have to go through it first. If you have any issues that you haven't dealt with, you'll be able to work through them as you participate."

I don't have any problems to deal with, I thought. To Hans I said, "I'll let you know next week." I quickly decided I didn't have any unresolved issues and I didn't have time to take the course. Yet the next Wednesday I heard myself telling him I'd take it!

Is this You, God? I wondered.

I sat in a circle with five other attendees, a facilitator, and a counselor. We were at the end of a long day. We had watched a video explaining the whys and wherefores of the many problems we faced in today's society. It focused in particular on the causes of family breakdowns and the effect these had on the children involved. The video described the function of healthy families and the role of a good mother and a good father and the impact of both on the children.

The counselor spoke, "I want each of you to pray and ask God to show you if there are any hurts that you are still holding onto from your childhood. If God reveals anything to you, do let us know and we will pray with you. You could unwittingly be depriving yourselves of all God has for you."

Goodness, I thought, *all these years as a Christian, surely I have it together by now.* I totally trusted in God and with Him I'd proved to be a woman full of confidence.

"Take your time," the counselor spoke again.

I squirmed; I felt uncomfortable and wanted to leave. Someone to my left started to cry and immediately the counselor and the facilitator were there with her. They huddled together and spoke so softly I couldn't hear what they were saying. What I could hear were the women's loud sobs and lots of nose blowing. Finally she left, nodding and smiling as the counselor said a few last words to her.

"Anyone else want to share?" the facilitator asked. *What I want is out of here*, I thought.

But I had a distinct feeling that I had to deal with something from way, way back. It couldn't be Sister St. Claire, Ada or Gardener Grimshaw; I remembered I had forgiven them soon after I'd become a Christian. I'd learned just as God forgave me so I had to forgive all who'd hurt me. I remembered how I'd had to ask God to help me forgive them. Then the counselor spoke again.

"Do each of you know how precious you are to God? Can you look back and say with confidence God ordained your very existence?"

"No I can't." The words were out of my mouth before I could think and quickly the counselor and facilitator brought their chairs close to mine. I started to cry. *What is it*, I wondered? I struggled for answers.

"Mary do you want to share anything?" the counselor asked. The floodgates burst and I poured out the story of my birth.

"Do you believe God ordained your existence?" he asked again.

"No I don't. I don't think I was ever meant to be." The counselor leaned toward me.

"Mary when you go home tonight I want you to ask God for answers—ask Him if He meant you to be." I grabbed a tissue and blew my nose. "Promise me you will, Mary."

"Okay," I whispered. He and the facilitator prayed with me and asked God to show me how special I was to Him. I said thank you and good-bye and then drove home.

I reviewed some of my notes that evening, watched the news, and thought about the promise I'd made to the counselor. But suppose I asked God, how would He let me know? Eventually I went upstairs and got ready for bed. *I have to ask Him*, I thought as I lay in the dark. I closed my eyes and said, "Dear God could you let me know if You meant me to be?" I waited for a thought or a Scripture to pop into my mind but instead I saw a bright yellow flower shaped like a tulip, but with the head flexed forward. The flower had hundreds of slender petals that overlapped each other; a fierce wind began to blow forcing some of the petals to the ground. I could see a tiny fetus inside the flower and I knew it was me. *How am I going to get out of there*, I wondered. A voice—a silent voice but somehow I heard it—spoke to me saying, "You were Mine from the moment of conception." At the same time a Scripture popped into my head *"Behold I hold you in the palm of my hand,"* and from the book of Isaiah, *"No weapon forged against you will prevail, you will refute every tongue that accuses you. This is the heritage of the servants of the Lord, and this is their vindication from Me, declares the Lord."*

I had believed long ago that there were no more tears to be shed—that the tears for the abuse, failed marriage, and hurts had all been spent. But the tears I shed that night left me exhausted and at the same time at peace with this amazing Jesus I'd come to know. I thought of the poem we had learned as children:

"Little Lamb who made thee
Dost thou know who made thee?
Gave thee life & bid thee feed...
Little Lamb who made thee
Dost thou know who made thee?

Little Lamb I'll tell thee,
Little Lamb I'll tell thee!
He is called by thy name,
For he calls himself a Lamb:
He is meek & he is mild,

He became a little child:
I a child & thou a lamb,
We are called by his name.
Little Lamb God bless thee.
Little Lamb God bless thee."

—William Blake:
Songs of Innocence and Experience, 1789.

28

The Search

Soon after the vision of the bright yellow flower, I recalled with exuberance that my favorite color had always been yellow! Now I had an urge to try and find family again. I wanted to know my origins. In the past I had searched on and off for many years. Knowing God meant me to exist gave me confidence and I felt sure He'd be with me in this venture.

I started the search in earnest in July 1999 and had a sizable file to prove it.

When Mario and I lived in England, I had been to Somerset House, where all marriages, births, and death records were kept at that time. I had my adoption certificate telling me Reverend Mother had adopted me January 26, 1937, when I was two years and five months. But what could I find out about my birth mother? I carried the family name, Melloy, which gave me some leverage and before long I obtained my birth certificate. Astonished, I discovered my mother had entered her husband Edward as my father. She had given birth to me in a private nursing home in Kent and had recorded the name of it and her place of residence on the certificate as well as her husband's occupation as that of a Missionary Society Traveling Lecturer—intriguing to say the least; nevertheless for me—valuable information.

Armed with this knowledge I now began my search. I started by going to the Internet and contacting people with the same surname—Melloy. I fired off several e-mails of inquiry and received a few responses. People were kind and wished me all the best. I even phoned the library in the sub-district of my birth forgetting that England's time was four hours ahead of Canada. I spoke to a lady who happened to be in the library after closing hours

"My you do have a story," she said, once I had explained the purpose of my call. "You won't believe this, but I was born in that same nursing home and you and I are about the same age! Just wait a moment dear and I'll do a quick run through the directory here."

She then gave me the names of all the Melloys in the district, their addresses and phone numbers and I immediately contacted them all. But all the letter writing, phone calls, and e-mails came to nothing. I posted messages on the Melloy genealogy board and had responses from as far away as Australia, but not one that led me to family.

Next, remembering Edward's occupation, I decided to contact churches in the region—my goal being to find out what denomination might have sent out "Missionary Traveling Lecturers." Ministers did not respond, but I continued to go through the churches in the region and came across a web page that caught my attention. Whoever had designed it knew Jesus. The content made it clear. It gave information about the Kennington United Reformed/Methodist Church in Kent. The web designer's name and e-mail appeared on the front page inviting visitors to the site to write. There were several links to other sites too, such as history of the church, its activities, and maps and directions. Deciding to e-mail right away, I wrote:

Dear Hugh,

Greetings from Canada: I am visiting churches in Kent via the Internet for a specific reason, but would first like to congratulate you on an excellent web page. It's obvious that you really KNOW Jesus. Me too! Praise His name.

I went on to give Hugh the pertinent information I had and asked if he might know the denomination that Edward, my mother's husband, had belonged to. I then continued:

> For some reason, I want to tell you more. Edward's wife, my mother, had an affair with one of the foreign students and that's how I came to be. Needless to say, the shame back then would have been hard to bear. My mother gave birth to me in a private nursing home and from there a Mother Superior, the head of an Anglican order of nuns, took me into her care, eventually adopting me.
>
> There is another twist to this story, the students were colored, as they were referred to back then, and so I am—coffee with the cream color! All my life I've known there are relatives out there and I've made attempts to find them. The Salvation Army did a search many years ago before I came to Canada. They definitely made inroads, but told me that I would be hurting others by pursuing this.
>
> However here I am, wanting to give my siblings, nephews, and nieces a hug. I know it would be a shock for them, but I'm praying God would give them kindness and love toward me.
>
> If there is any way that you might be able to help in speeding up my search, I would be grateful for your input.
>
> Sincerely, in anticipation,
> Mary

Hugh replied immediately, giving me the names and addresses of Melloys in the area. He wrote at the end of his e-mail,

> Which part of Canada are you from? I visited Vancouver Island, British Columbia once.
> Kind regards,
> Hugh

In my response I told him where I lived and that Daniela and I had visited Butchart Gardens on Vancouver Island. I also said, "I hope you don't mind, but I noticed a couple of spelling errors on your website. I'm sure you'll want to correct them..."

He e-mailed back, "thanks for the corekshuns-easily dun!" I realized God had connected me with a fun and congenial person. I first connected with Hugh in March 2000 and through the many e-mail exchanges that followed, I learned he was an Electronic Design Engineer and also a local Methodist Preacher. And that he and his wife Jane had a young son. Hugh sent information and websites he thought might be useful and also put me in touch with Levina, a genealogist friend.

Levina did some digging and over time was able to locate and send to me the marriage certificate of my mother and her husband and the birth certificates of their two children. Next I asked Levina if she could find out if my brother and sister had married. Information showed up about my sister, but nothing on my brother. My sister had apparently married and had two children. I acquired her son John's birth certificate, then asked Levina to check to see if he also had married and found that yes, he had.

My brother remained a mystery. No marriage record could be found and Levina and I surmised that maybe he had died in the war. Neither could any contact information for my sister or her family be found. I had proof of their existence, but where were they? The search had come to a dead end, almost as if the family had fallen off the face of the earth.

In January 2001, I closed the file and put it on my shelf. However I couldn't let it go for long. I kept thinking about Hazil's happy outcome, and in February 2001 I sent a letter to the Salvation Army with a copy of my file. I asked if they would consider doing a family search for me even though I had been adopted since their policy at that time did not include searches for adopted children.

Months went by and no response. In July, I contacted them again and apparently there had been a change in administration with my file continuing to lay somewhere in a pile. The person I spoke to assured me, however, they would carry out a search and inform me of any progress. I asked God to let them find my family and left it at that.

29

Reflecting on Fran

Spring 1998:

I made my way through Strathroy Hospital and entered the ward where Fran had been admitted.

"Didn't you want to help with the packing?" I teased, as I walked to her bedside. She chuckled.

Fran had called me a couple of weeks previous to say that she and Al were selling Gilead and moving back into the city. "I won't need the planners anymore Mary; we're retiring and we feel it best to be in the city for health care." For several years I had given Fran a planner for Christmas, a big one that she could make notes in as well as record all the retreat bookings.

"I fractured the long bone in my hip. Can you believe it, just stepping out of my slip."

"It's so easily done. How does it feel?"

"Not too bad," she said with a smile. "The incision is sore yet."

I looked at Fran and thought that in all the years I'd known her I'd never heard her complain, grumble, or say an unkind word about anyone. I remembered the year before when her daughter ran a second time for mayor of London and had a landslide victory, but in all the excitement Fran had taken a nasty fall, tripping over television cables as she hurried toward the area where Dianne readied for an interview with the media. She fell off the platform to the floor several feet below, crushing her facial bones. I had worked as a volunteer on Dianne's campaign and she called me the next morning to tell me what had transpired.

"The doctor is saying that Mom will have to have reconstructive facial surgery, with titanium plates inserted," Dianne said, "but I think that is so drastic. Will you pray that she'll heal? I believe that already," she added.

And of course I believed with Dianne, as did others, and Fran healed without surgical intervention. But now Fran was back in hospital with a broken hip.

"Do you know when you'll be discharged?" I asked Fran.

"The physiotherapist is going to start me on exercises tomorrow."

"That's good. You make sure you toe the line now!" We chatted awhile longer and then I said I had to get back home. I loved the fact that she too had prayed the prayer that made the difference. So for us to bow our heads and talk to God about issues that concerned us was as natural as breathing. Before I left the hospital we held hands and prayed. I prayed for a speedy recovery for Fran and she prayed for Al, that God would provide the necessary help with the move back to town.

"Once we're settled in you have to come over to the house," Fran said.

"Of course," I said, as I gave her a hug.

Fran's discharge came soon enough and with physiotherapy she regained some of her strength and mobility. Before long I phoned Fran to see when it would be convenient for me to visit. "Come for lunch," she said, "How's tomorrow?"

The next day arriving at the house I met Jean, a competent lady who had moved in to help Al and Fran in the running of their home. Fran's general health had suffered and the following year saw her back in hospital with a serious chest infection that nearly took her life. Only family was allowed to visit. However, once she rallied and transferred to St. Mary's Hospital, I visited her there. Once again she recovered and went home.

Unfortunately Fran's health again caused her trouble—this time even more serious as she faced cancer. One day as I visited in her living room, she said, "You know Mary, I want to see Annie grow up," as she spoke with tears in her eyes of Dianne's daughter, her only grandchild.

"Oh, Fran." I knelt by her chair and held her. "I'm sure you will."

Lord, please touch Fran and grant her good health, I silently prayed.

A few days later Al called me to say Fran had been admitted to hospital again. She had had several doctors' appointments and tests. Major surgery now seemed likely but in the end attempts to build up her strength for the surgical procedure failed. Fran was transferred to hospice care at Parkwood Hospital and there I visited with her several times.

The time came when Dianne returned from Washington and Dianne's sister Kelsey came from Langley, British Columbia. And I did not visit anymore. On July 3rd, 2001, Dianne called to tell me Fran had passed away. I knew with a certainty that she had gone to heaven and that I would see her again.

Many people attended the funeral service at London Gospel Temple. I looked around and realized how many people gentle Fran had endeared herself to, and I was happy to be in that number.

July 6, 2001, an excerpt from my journal:

"Well Lord, it's 4:50 p.m. and I'm in the park. I love it here. There's a fair wind blowing but the sun is hot! As you know I've been at London Gospel Temple for Fran's funeral. Fran's with You now and I know that without a doubt, but the point is I'll miss her and even more to the point so will her dear husband. Comfort him oh, Lord and use me to be a comfort to him in which ever way you see fit..."

30

Winds of Change

I sat with Nancy, hearing the excitement in her voice as she shared with me about her new love. Cutting into the chicken on my plate, I popped a piece into my mouth and between chews said, "Tell me more." Nancy grinned—that dreamy type of grin that says, *I'm in love with a wonderful guy.*

We were having dinner at my place, sitting in the dining area. The sunshine streamed through the slats of the Venetian blinds.

"I had just done a consultation on a patient," Nancy said, "and I sat at the nurses station charting, when along comes the doctor who oversees the patients there. He was so pleasant, introduced himself, and so on." She grinned again. "I think he might be the one."

"How long have we been praying?" I asked, "It seems like we just started." We figured it was in the spring of 2001. Nancy had read T.D. Jakes' book, *Woman Thou Art Loosed.* In it he had focused on the rights of women to have freedom in Jesus. As Nancy shared, we realized we had the right to ask God for Christian husbands and we decided we would pray every day from that point forward for the husbands that we didn't yet know. Our excitement knew no bounds and we were convinced that somehow God would bring them. We were in August now and it seemed God had brought Nancy's husband-to-be into her life.

I recalled the day we decided to start praying. We had joined hands and we prayed one for the other. Nancy had finished praying for me; even so we sat quietly with eyes closed. Suddenly, she spoke with conviction. "Mary I saw in my mind's eye a tall, distinguished man with silver-gray hair for you." Convinced, I determined to pray for this man from that day on. I often went to Springbank Park and there I'd sit and talk to God through my journaling. On one occasion I wrote, "How's my husband today Lord? I pray all is well with him." Another time, "How is my future husband today Lord? Is he well? I pray Your hand upon him for good. Be with him wherever he is. Sometimes as You well know I'm impatient for You to bring him to me. How long will I wait, oh God? How long?"

Soon after this entry, my friend Dee called to tell me she had been praying for me and believed God would answer my prayer before long.

I talked to God about many issues in my journal—my children, my friends, like Val and Carolyn, Nancy and Dee, and my sister Hazil. I told God how Val would like a husband, and Hazil, who had been widowed for sometime, would like one too. I loved communing with God this way.

Nancy spoke. "It's just about three months," she said, "since we started praying."

"What an amazing God, Nancy. I know soon He'll bring mine into my life. I wonder where I'll meet him."

We finished our meal and sat out in my little back yard to have a tea. Nancy told me more about Paul, the doctor she couldn't stop talking about. The evening ended, and as always, we prayed before she left.

The next morning as had happened more than once, Al Haskett popped into my mind, not so much him, but his name. I frowned. *Could this be You Lord?* I really didn't want to connect with him; it just didn't seem right now that Fran had gone. And besides what would I say? He had said to me at the funeral he hoped we'd still be friends; however I thought he had plenty of friends who would be visiting him. But the thought persisted.

After deliberating with myself, I decided to call him and ask if he would like to go out to Springbank Park. "I go there often and write in my journal," I said. "I could pick you up—I practically drive past your place." I knew he was to have a hip replacement and that's why I offered to drive. He seemed genuinely pleased.

At the park, Al talked a lot about Fran. He had brought some of the sympathy cards he had received and gave them to me to read. I mostly asked questions so he could verbalize his feelings. He choked up a bit and so did I. The next day I wrote in my journal, "I took Al Haskett out to Springbank. We had a pleasant visit. He is a dear man. I pray things will work out for him regarding his home situation." Al had mentioned he did not know whether he would stay in his house or not.

In August, Hazil took me to Port Stanley for my birthday. The drive was an hour out of London. Driving through the little fishing village, we passed an array of boats moored in the river and bobbing gently on the water. We parked and browsed the boutiques with their fine merchandise and then had dinner at The Kettle Creek Inn, a charming restaurant with an appetizing cuisine. Later that month, Val and I drove to Braeside camp for some of the services. Again I thought of calling Al to see how he fared.

"Would you like to go out to Springbank Park again?" I asked.

"I'd love to." He sounded more cheerful than last time. And I felt glad for him. And so it was that once in a while I visited with Al.

The summer came to an end. I had enjoyed my outings and fellowship with friends. Still I prayed for the husband that was out there somewhere. For Al, I called and asked if he would like to go to Port Stanley for a picnic before cooler days prevailed. We did that and it turned out to be an extraordinary day. The next morning I sat down and wrote to the Lord in my journal:

"Dear Lord, what a day yesterday—Al Haskett told me he loves and admires me and he hopes eventually that we might be a couple. This declaration came as a total shock! He says that he realizes Fran has only been gone a short while but he wanted to tell me how he felt. I looked into his face and saw love, hope, and longing..."

I wrote on and on, telling God I saw him as an elderly gentleman, and all the negatives I saw in such a union. Then I wrote "Yet Al is everything I asked of You. He's gentle, kind, intelligent, and humorous. Is this the man You've chosen for me Lord? I feel very emotional right now, fearful, overwhelmed and unsure. I'm going to leave this at Your throne of grace. Please advise, dear Lord."

I reflected on the unfolding of the day and remembered as I drove away from Al's house, he stood at the door waving good-bye. "Oh, my goodness," I said over and over again as I clutched the wheel, "I have to call Nancy and tell her, he's in my life—the tall, distinguished man with the silver-gray hair!"

I had never thought one way or the other about Al's appearance or about Al really. I had seen him at Gilead many times and sat with him and Fran for meals. Mostly I spent time with Fran, while Al took care of their twenty-six acre property. I remembered the first time I saw him—he brought an armful of logs into the large lounge area where our women's group met for Bible study, sing-song, food, and fun. He stoked up the fire, while Fran gave three of us women a quick overview of the kitchen area.

"This is where you can make the tea and coffee," she said. Fran then confirmed the time she would have breakfast ready for us the next morning. "Just call me if you have any questions," she said with a warm smile.

But now, all these years later, what a change of events; I needed to talk to God about this and I needed to know if He approved. *Had He orchestrated this?* I kept writing in my journal:

"September 3. A myriad of emotions continue to swirl, butterflies in my stomach, loving thoughts toward Al and at the same time, 'Is this okay with you Lord?'"

"I want you to see him differently now." *Dear Lord is that you?*

I wrote the next day:

"The more I think, the more amazed I am, of all the women he must know that his dear heart is toward me. 'You know God, I cried just now thinking about it. It's overwhelming and now tears threaten again. I'm sure this is of You Lord. Continue to guide and direct I pray.'"

Talking to God through my journaling continued unabated for days. I told Him about my feelings, my elation, then my doubts and He listened to it all, doubtless with a smile.

Later Al took me out to dinner. I guess it was our first official date. The enormity of all that had transpired began to take root. By this time we knew it was God's plan. We discussed our children and their reactions to our news. How would Al's daughters, Dianne and Kelsey feel? We prayed, asking God to prepare their hearts and for us to be sensitive to their needs.

Late September I invited Al to my home for dinner and there he met Mike and Dave and they told me they approved! "He's a handsome man into the bargain," Mike said.

October came and Al flew to Washington to spend the month with Dianne and her husband Jack and daughter Annie, by which time Al had told his family and my children all knew. Dear Dianne embraced the news. She told us that it did not catch her entirely by surprise and she related an unusual story. When she had visited her former law firm in London several years earlier, the office manager, Gail Twohey, shared with her that she had just had a strange dream. In the dream, Dianne's dad, Al, had been at the office Christmas party with his wife, but the name of his wife was Mary! Dianne told Al and me that she had often thought about that dream and wondered if it was foretelling of the possibility that her dad might outlive her mom and remarry some day.

But for Kelsey it was not so easy—she had not had sufficient time to grieve the loss of her mother and she urged us to wait. We decided to do so, assuring her we would wait until the next summer to wed.

When Al returned from Washington, we agreed to make it official and let friends know of our intentions. Hazil invited us to dinner and took pictures of us grinning from ear to ear. Al agreed to attend services with me at Royal View, my home church, and there I proudly introduced him to many of my friends.

Christmas day my dear children were with me along with Mike's lovely fiancée, Kelly, and her mom and grandma, and of course Hazil. Daniela, as always, did an excellent job of preparing the table. I had written in my journal "Martha Stewart step aside!"

On Boxing Day, Al came with his family to my home, giving everyone opportunity to get acquainted.

On New Years Eve I wrote in my journal:

"Al picked me up at 5:30 p.m. We drove to the Riverview Restaurant. He had booked a table for 6:30 p.m. We both looked good, Al in his new jacket and slacks, white shirt, and dark red tie. What a darling, handsome man. I wore my elegant dark maroon suit with a soft champagne colored shell blouse and the pearl earrings he had given me. I looked pretty, at least that's what Al told me and Kelsey told me the same thing later on at the church. (Kelsey, the head of the Modern Languages Department at Trinity Western University, was home from British Columbia.)

'Well Lord, thank You for our wonderful evening. Thank You for the red rose Al gave me and thank You for the engagement ring tied to the bow—and the beautiful service at the church and pastor's sermon. It was good that he reminded us of the processes You set out for all of us. Most of all I thank You for Kelsey. I experienced her genuine love and acceptance of me today and I'm in awe of Your wonderful working in this situation. Thank You that You've placed such a love in my heart for dear Kelsey. Bless her Lord and grant her her heart's desires. Amen.'"

31

More Than One Wedding

On Friday May 10, 2002, my eldest son Mike married his sweetheart Kelly. Al and I had our date set for June 22nd.

Long before I knew which direction God had me headed, I had decided to sell my three-bedroom condominium and move into a small apartment. No one had shown any interest and the months had slipped by. Now with my pending marriage, I needed to sell my home. Al and a family friend, Cliff, determined some paint in the dining area and some minor sprucing up in the kitchen might help and it did, with the very next viewers putting in an offer. I had to be out of my home a month before the wedding and my friend Val invited me to stay at her home. Then for the last week I moved in with Hazil. She was to be my maid of honor, help me prepare for the great day and ride to the church with me. And on that day, Cliff drove us to the church and helped us out of the car.

My family greeted me with hugs, kisses, and compliments in the foyer.

"Mom you look beautiful."

I did not realize my own excitement until Mike took both my hands bent down, and said with quiet authority. "Mom, listen to me, I know you've counseled and calmed people many times—now I want you to take some of your own advice." He shook me gently,

"Mom listen to me and look at me." I couldn't stop giggling. And Mike wouldn't let go until he had me under control. Pastor Fess, Hazil and the rest of my family waited patiently while Mike dealt with Mommy!

Chris said to me later, "You know Mom, Mike and I thought we might have to send for the men in the white coats!"

The ceremony went well. Kelsey played the piano softly prior to the service. Mike escorted me down the aisle and Hazil followed behind. Chris and Dave ushered. Kelly and Sue, my daughters-in-law and Jasmine and Annie, our granddaughters—mine and Al's respectively—greeted people at the door. Dianne read the Scripture and Jack, her husband, was best man. My friends Val and Judy Fess sang a duet. Judy had suggested "Great is Thy Faithfulness," and a more appropriate hymn could not have been chosen. Her husband, Pastor Gary Fess, led a beautiful service. Daniela and Chris' girlfriend Patrice, both able photographers, took all our wedding pictures. Our day of enchantment concluded with dinner at the Riverview Restaurant with our families and close friends, including Paul and Nancy who married the following year.

Nancy asked me to read the Scripture passage at their wedding and my tall, distinguished man with the silver-gray hair asked the blessing at their reception.

Later Hazil had a whirlwind romance with Jack, a charming gentleman from her church. Her sons and a few close friends attended her wedding. I was her maid of honor. And so God honored our prayers and blessed each one of us with husbands.

Al and I had been married for two and a half months when someone called from the Salvation Army in September 2002 to say they had found my sister.

32

Connections

We listened to the announcer's voice on our portable radio. "There is a power outage in south-west London from the current storm. Trees have been uprooted and telephone poles are down. Police advise people to stay in their homes."

I watched fierce winds through our kitchen window, whipping the trees this way and that. I said to Al, "The sycamore tree is having a heyday." Al chuckled; he knew about my love-hate relationship with our sycamore tree. It was an unusual species that constantly shed bark as if playing ping-pong and not only that—it cheerfully threw its unwanted branches all over our yard and into the rock garden. With the help of the storm, it was truly in its element.

We didn't need any advice to stay put. Al found a Coleman camping stove and we managed to rustle up a meal. By the time we'd finished, the winds had subsided and he suggested we sit out on the deck. I stacked the dishes in the sink saying, "They can wait till later." As Al opened the screen door, the phone rang and I picked it up. It was Maria, a dear friend who had moved away from London.

"Maria, how are you? Where are you?" I said.

"Ken and I are in London and wondered if we could come over for a visit?"

"Of course, we'd love to see you."

Reflecting on my relationship with Ken and Maria brought back many happy memories. They had attended Royal View Church for several years until they moved to Bowmanville following Ken's retirement. We had sung in the choir together and I had sat under Ken's teaching in Sunday school class. My youngest son Chris had a great friendship with their three daughters. And I had been privileged to be a guest at each of the girl's weddings, as well as a guest in their lovely home.

Once Ken and Maria arrived, we settled on the deck and caught up on news.

"By the way," Ken asked, "how's the family search going?"

"I found my sister."

"That's so exciting," Maria leaned forward in her chair. "Are you going to visit?"

"We already did last September," Al said.

"And?" she said, her eyes sparkling.

I told Ken and Maria the whole story and the disappointment of my sister's decision. "She doesn't want the family to know about me and I don't think I can violate her wishes."

Al interjected. "Mary, remember the conversation with John? It sounded as if your great-nephew was a pastor."

"That's right." I turned to my friends. "I had a brief conversation with him on the phone. He went to the same college as your girls. Do you think they might have known him?"

"Well you never know," Ken said. "Give me his name and I'll ask Carie to check the alumni list." Eventually Ken and Maria said their good-byes, promising to get back to me with information about my great-nephew.

After Ken and Maria's visit, I pulled out my family search file and reviewed the many e-mails back and forth with Hugh. Returning from the United States subsequent to the visit with my sister I had written:

Dear Hugh,

We are back from the States. We stayed at a hotel and each day of our four-day visit we spent time with my sister. She is 90 years old! She was a young married woman and carrying her own child when I was conceived. I thank God for her clarity of thought and that she was able to fill in many of the gaps.

To learn about my mother was somewhat disappointing, she being 'the life and soul of the party' type of character. You will recall she had an affair with one of the students—my father. He was indeed a law student from West Africa and 20 years her junior. I always imagined she suffered giving up her baby, but instead she sought to abort me, but was told she was too far along with the pregnancy...

My mother and her husband were with the Baptist Society of London. They traveled throughout England raising funds for the society. Apparently she played the piano and sang duets with her husband, and as we already knew, housed overseas students from the West Indies and West Africa. The students were in transit... Mum and her husband found them lodgings near the university.

At the time of my arrival, Edward, Mum's husband, had a good friend who happened to know Reverend Mother and that's how I came to be placed with her.

The family was devastated with all that happened and poor Edward suffered dreadfully. He and mum separated. He died at an early age but Mum lived till three months shy of her 100th birthday...

I thought Hugh might be interested to know about the vision of the bright yellow flower and I described that experience to him. At the end I wrote:

Then a voice, not really audible, said "You were Mine from the moment of conception." I'm crying, what can I say, only praise to the God of my salvation...

Hugh, enough for now, I thank God for His kindness to me and the many blessings He has showered upon me. I know God blesses you too. There is much more to tell, but I will close for now.

Hugh wrote back the next day:

Hello Mary,

It sounds as if you have had a tremendous and probably quite emotional time.

Your value to those around you and to God is quite independent of your parents, and I'm delighted that you have received confirmation of this through a vision. After all, our Lord Himself was a child conceived out of wedlock! While the circumstances around Christ' birth are rather different, one can imagine the social stigma that Mary, mother of Jesus must have experienced...

Just because your mother wanted to have an abortion, doesn't mean that it wasn't hard for her to part with you. There is a tremendous bond between a mother and child, which goes far beyond intellectual understanding...

Hugh shared a few things about his family and closed with,

Bye for now
God bless
Hugh.

I spent a couple of hours reviewing all the correspondence in my file. It troubled me that after all the efforts to find my family and finally meeting my sister, she had shut the door in my face.

Several weeks went by and I hadn't received any word from Ken and Maria, so I e-mailed them. Ken responded right away with an apology. He thought he had already sent me the news that my great-nephew, Peter, had indeed been in a class ahead of the girls.

Now I had enough information to track him down via the Internet. But my sister's wish that I remain unknown held me back. *Did I have the right to go against her wishes?* I wrote down his name, address, and phone number on a piece of paper and tucked it into my purse. I'd have to think about it.

33

Conquering Fear

"I'm home," Al called as he came into the house through the garage door.

"How was your swim today?"

"Good. I did my usual half hour." he said, giving me a hug. I finished getting our breakfast ready then we sat down, joined hands and Al asked the blessing.

"You know something?"

"Not till you tell me," he said with a smile.

"I wish I could swim; if I could, then we could go together."

"Why don't you take lessons?"

Memories of Ada, holding me down in the bath water, and children dragging me into the sea while I howled in terror, immediately came to mind. "I guess I'm too old and too scared now."

"You should give it a try, sweetheart," Al said, "Why don't you check the community programs?"

I thought about his suggestion on and off over the next few days. I visualized myself gliding like a dolphin through the water and I'd smile at the thought. However, a large body of water with nothing to hold onto and the possibility of drowning did not appeal in the least and I dismissed the idea.

Al went swimming early mornings three times a week. I'd say a sleepy good-bye, roll over and snuggle back under the blankets for a while before getting up. Each time he came home he'd tell me about people he had talked to in the pool and the friendly banter that often ensued, mostly from the many women who gathered there for an exercise class. "That's it," I announced one morning, "I'm going to check the community programs and take swimming lessons."

With my mind made up, I phoned and booked six sessions for adult beginners—definitely where I fitted in!

There were six of us standing waist deep in the pool. The instructor gave us a brief overview of the techniques of swimming. "Now the first thing I want you to do is float face down in the water, stretch your arms out in front of you and paddle with your feet."

"Face in the water—you mean I have to get my hair wet!"

"That's the first thing you need to do if you're going to swim. Let me show you," said our instructor as he glided effortlessly across the pool. He then stood in the water and said, "Breathe in before you start." Some of the others got going right away. I swished my hands back and forth and wondered what on earth had possessed me to even venture this far. I attempted a smile at the guy standing next to me and surmised he was even more nervous than me. Our instructor focused on another lady who made gallant efforts to get on with it. But not for long and soon he urged me, mind you very gently, to go for it! "I promise you won't sink," he added.

"Okay. Come on Mary," I said out loud. *Help me Lord, not to be afraid!* And with that, I breathed in and down I went. I kicked and felt myself moving forward. Then up I came, wiping the water from my face. Al had come with me and sat on the bench cheering me on.

"That's great sweetheart, good for you." He made me feel like the champion of champions and his encouragement kept me going over the next six weeks. I didn't exactly learn to swim but by the end of that time I was kicking with my feet and doing my own version of the breaststroke with my arms! Most importantly, I learned to stay afloat.

I signed up for six more private lessons with the purpose of mastering at least one stroke. "Push, kick and glide, push kick and glide," the young instructor kept repeating as I made valiant efforts to master the dynamics of the breaststroke. At the end of the week, I probably would have been awarded an 'A' for effort! True to my resolve, I started going to the pool with Al and instructed myself in push, kick and glide, with Al encouraging me all the way until I had it down pat. One day he went a little further into the deep end and said, "Do you want to swim to me?" I barely did so, but then had a moment of panic, turned around and swam to the shallower part of the pool, all the while telling myself to keep calm.

I enjoy going to the pool in the mornings with Al. And I love the way he never tries to tell me where I should swim, but always tells me he's proud of me for being there. Sometimes when we're driving home he says, "McDonald's or McHaskett's for breakfast?" And we both think an occasional Egg McMuffin is okay.

As for my swimming, I did venture into the deep end again on one or two occasions, but then settled for the four-foot section. Maybe, just maybe, I'll take that next step one day and swim freely in the deeper waters.

34

Family Again

Thoughts of Ken and Maria's visit and the reviewing of my file brought to the forefront of my mind my sister's wishes that my existence be kept from family. It bothered me that she could hold such control over me.

I don't want the family to know about you...poor daddy...seeing you a brown baby. Snatches of my sister's comments came back to me. I wondered about my brother James. My sister had told me James had been killed in a freak accident at age fourteen. He had been wrestling with a school friend and had tripped, falling backwards, impaling himself on a wrought iron fence. What would he have been like if he'd lived? Would he have been more accepting? Would he have had children who would have welcomed me? Unfortunately I'd never know. And my niece also died in her early years. Would she or any of her off-spring have welcomed me?

The thoughts kept coming and in the end I made a decision to speak to my pastor. Al and I were now attending London Gospel Temple since it was closer to our home. I gave Pastor Smith a brief synopsis of my story and asked for his opinion. "You know," he said, "I've dealt with similar situations. If you like I will call him and then he can decide whether he wants to meet you."

My hopes soared. "Thank you Pastor," I said as I gave him my great-nephew's phone number.

My pastor called me on the Monday. "Hello Mary, I've spoken to your nephew. Needless to say the news surprised him, but he said to tell you his daughter is getting married on Saturday and after the wedding he'll be in touch."

"That's good news, Pastor. Do you think he really will?"

"Oh, yes," Pastor said, "I'm sure of it."

"Al," I yelled down into the basement. "My great-nephew's going to call me."

"What did you say?" Al stood at the bottom of the stairs. Laughing, I started down and repeated the news when the phone rang again. "I'll get it," I said, scurrying back up.

"Hello," I said, a little breathlessly.

"Is this Mary?"

"That's me," I responded.

"Mary, your pastor just called me." My pulse quickened and I gulped. "I'm Peter, your great-nephew. I think! Can you tell me something about yourself?"

"Well yes" I said, not knowing where to start. "I thought you weren't going to call until next week." He explained he was in his office and felt he had to call right away.

"I understand you've met my dad and grandma. How did you find out that we're related?"

I took a deep breath and gave Peter a brief overview of my story and he said as soon as the wedding was over he'd call again. I finished by saying, "There's one thing you should know, I'm 'coffee with the cream color.'"

I heard him chuckling. "That Grandma!" he said, "Bye for now, Aunt Mary."

I put the phone down and wiped tears from my eyes. Al had come up from the basement. He looked at me and said, "Tell me."

I told him about my conversation with Peter. "But he called me Aunt," I said, "He called me Aunt. He didn't question our relationship. He believed." Al came to me and hugged me. "That's wonderful sweetheart," he said.

An hour later the phone rang again. "Aunt Mary, it's Peter. I've told my wife and two children about you and we want you and your husband to come to the wedding on Saturday." I stood there stunned; when I recovered, joy bells were ringing in my head. "Aunt Mary?"

"Yes Peter, are you sure?" He assured me he was sure and I said, "Thank you so much. I'll talk to Al and we'll let you know."

"You tell Uncle Al we want you both to come. I realize it's a long journey, but you could leave on Friday or even Thursday and then get rested up in time for the wedding."

Al had no moments of hesitation. "Of course we're going," he said.

Early on the Thursday morning, we started out on our second journey to Utica. We crossed the border at Buffalo and took the same route as before, Interstate 90 east through New York State. Peter had given us the location of a couple of motels close to his church and we had arranged to meet him there on the Friday. We pulled into the parking lot at the same time. With a big smile and a handshake, he greeted us and we entered his church, sat in a pew and talked. He shook his head several times as we shared. The fact that his father and grandma had reacted in the way they had amazed him. "To think they never told us," he said.

"How do you think your dad will react when he sees me at the wedding?" I asked.

"I don't know," Peter said, "but that's his problem, not ours." He got up. "I should be off. There are several last minute matters to be attended to." We said our good-byes and Al and I went back to our motel for a rest before dinner.

On the wedding day we entered the church and slipped into a seat toward the back. People noticed us and greeted us with smiles and nods. Eventually a lady came over to us. "Are you Aunt Mary?" she asked. I acknowledged that I was and thrilled at the warm reception people were giving us.

My great-great-niece made a beautiful bride. Her father—my great-nephew—and his close friend from Bible college days officiated at the wedding.

During the reception my nephew—my sister's son—came to say hello and introduced his wife. He didn't show any anger at me being there and was quite friendly and gracious.

On Sunday morning, we went to my great-nephew's church for the service. My joy knew no bounds when he announced to the congregation, "God has blessed me abundantly this week. I have gained a son-in-law and also He brought an aunt to me that I didn't know I had. And the most wonderful part is that she knows the Lord. Will you all welcome my Aunt Mary and Uncle Al from Canada?"

I'm sure no one ever smiled a broader smile than me that day except perhaps my tall, distinguished man with the silver-gray hair. The congregation applauded and many came and greeted us with hugs and handshakes.

My great-nephew, his wife, and their friends took us out to lunch after the service. I'm convinced that God smiled upon the events of that weekend. After all, He had granted me my heart's desire to know and receive acceptance from a blood relative, and most of all, from one who had prayed the prayer that made the difference.

As Al and I traveled along Interstate 90 and made our way back home, my heart sang with the joy of all that had transpired. I wondered if my precious Reverend Mother might be privy to the events of her Mary's life. I relaxed, leaned back in my car seat, closed my eyes, and saw her smiling face once more.

Will Vaus

MY FATHER WAS A GANGSTER
The Jim Vaus Story

One of the most fascinating conversion stories of the 20th century—the dramatic life story of Jim Vaus, former associate to America's underworld.

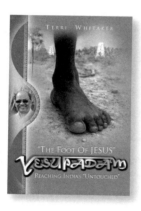

Terri Whitaker

YESUPADAM
Reaching India's Untouched

Yesupadam is the amazing story of God's miraculous work through an Untouchable Indian believer in Jesus and his Love-n-Care ministry in eastern India.

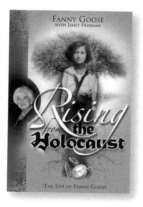

Fanny Goose
with Janet Fridman

RISING FROM THE HOLOCAUST
The Life of Fanny Goose

The astonishing real life story of an indomitable young Jewish girl who miraculously survives the horrors of Hitler's plot to destroy her people and goes on to live a joyful life.

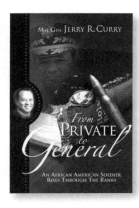

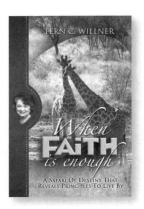

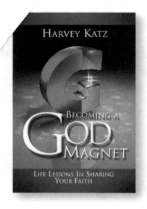

Harvey Katz

BECOMING A GOD MAGNET
The Secret to Sharing Your Faith
Book and **Study & Discussion Guide**

Harvey Katz's book *Becoming a God Magnet* is a practical, effective guide to evangelism. The *Study & Discussion Guide* is ideal for church or home groups willing to learn and share successful methods of personal evangelism.

Howard Katz

SEVEN ESSENTIAL RELATIONSHIPS
How To Pass God's Crucial Tests

The author uses the seven stages in the creation of a clay vessel, as well as an exposition of the life of Joseph, to illustrate each of the seven crucial tests that every believer must pass.

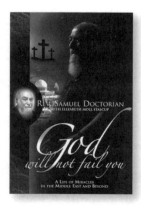

Rev. Samuel Doctorian
with Elizabeth Moll Stalcup, Ph.D.

GOD WILL NOT FAIL YOU
A Life of Miracles in the Middle East and Beyond

The miraculous life story of Rev. Samuel Doctorian, the renowned evangelist used mightily by God in the Middle East and around the world.

www.BelieveBooks.com